THIS GARDENING BOOK BELONGS TO:

_____

HARDINESS ZONE:

_____

ISBN: 9798739488503

Independently published

wink eye press

THE COMPLETE GARDEN PLANNER JOURNAL and LOGBOOK

PLAN, ORGANIZE and LOG ALL THE GREENERY IN YOUR LIFE

FOR FULL-SIZED GARDENS

CONTENTS

This Complete Garden Planner, Journal and Logbook includes:

20 Garden Layout Planner Sheets
This is a spot to work on some landscaping design: plot out what to plant in the front or back of your house. These layout sheets can also be used to plan your herb, vegetable, or floral planters.

80 Plant Logbook Entries
These plant logbook entries are flexible for all plantings: vegetables, herbs, indoor houseplants, shrubs, trees, showcase ornamental plants, and others. Nothing too serious to fill out, just the important details (plant type, size, light and soil requirements, maintenance, and also includes a space to sketch the plant or attach a photo).

30 Container Designer Sheets
This section of the book helps to keep track of all the different plant combinations that work well in each indoor/outdoor container or hanging basket so that your choices can be repeated for the next season. It also helps to design the color scheme so that it can complement the color of the container — includes space to sketch the plants inside the container or attach a photo of a successful container design.

20 Scheduler Sheets
This Scheduler section is flexible and can be used:
◇ As a Garden Maintenance Book (e.g. when to prune, mulch, or fertilize)
◇ To follow Blooming — Fruit/Harvest Activity
◇ Schedule the Planting Tasks (when to plant Vegetable Seeds, Bulbs, Tubers), or
◇ Track Color/Flowering Activity (to ensure that there is something interesting happening all the time) — all year round.

30 Journal Entries
This Garden Journal helps to keep track of gardening activities, garden inspiration ideas for next year, and for concepts that you saw at the local flower and garden show. Comes with garden-specific quotes.

GARDEN LAYOUT PLANNER SHEETS

HOW TO USE

Garden Layout Planner Sheets

Use these grids to plot out plantings in a variety of ways. The grid comes with a north arrow so you can determine which parts of the garden have the most sun and shade. Here are some examples of ways that the grids can be used:

◇ Keep track of the landscaping design in the front and backyard

◇ Plan future garden store purchases to see which plants would complement the yard and what available light there is next to taller trees/shrubs

◇ Use the grids to plan herb, vegetable, or floral planters for each season

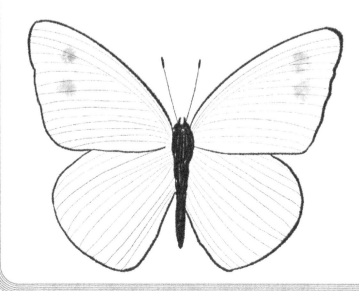

GARDEN LAYOUT

GARDEN LAYOUT

GARDEN LAYOUT

GARDEN LAYOUT

GARDEN LAYOUT

GARDEN LAYOUT

GARDEN LAYOUT

GARDEN LAYOUT

GARDEN LAYOUT

GARDEN LAYOUT

GARDEN LAYOUT

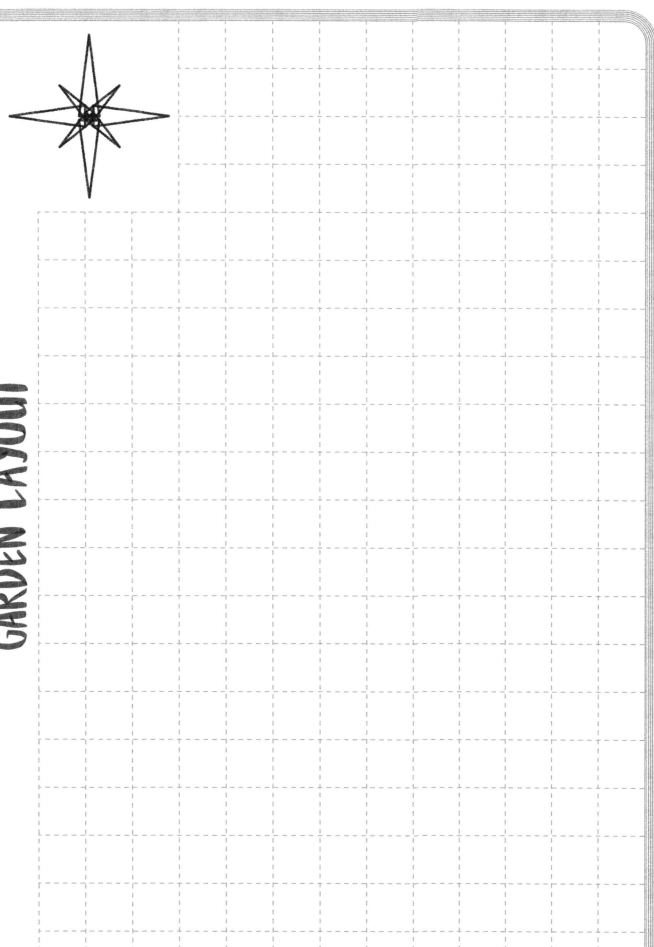

GARDEN LAYOUT

GARDEN LAYOUT

GARDEN LAYOUT

GARDEN LAYOUT

GARDEN LAYOUT

GARDEN LAYOUT

GARDEN LAYOUT

GARDEN LAYOUT

GARDEN LAYOUT

PLANT LOGBOOK

HOW TO USE

Plant Logbook Entries

These plant logbook entries are flexible for all plantings and have been designed so that the basics are captured — nothing too serious to fill out for the beginner gardener or hobby gardener. Features of the plant logbook include:

◇ Keeping track of any type of plant — check all the boxes that apply: vegetables, herbs, indoor houseplants, shrubs, trees, showcase ornamental plants, and others

◇ Enter the basic information that comes with the tag from the store — for example height, width, plant spacing, and light requirements

◇ A space has been set aside to sketch or paste photos so that the plants are easy to decipher when flipping through each page

◇ Additional writing blanks were also created so that care notes can also be included, such as pruning, pest and weed control, propagation, and fertilizer requirements

PLANT LOGBOOK

Plant Name (Common): _____

Genus Name: _____

☐ Bulb ☐ Herb ☐ Vegetable ☐ Shrub ☐ Tree ☐ Flower ☐ Indoor

☐ Rhizome ☐ Seedling ☐ Perennial ☐ Annual ☐ Biennial ☐ Outdoor

☐ Tuber ☐ Bare Root ☐ Vine ☐ Ornamental ☐ Fruit ☐ Groundcover

Attracts: _____

Resists: _____

Special Features: _____

Location Placed: _____

Date Planted: _____

Date Germinated: _____

Light Requirements:

☐ Shade ☐ Partial Sun ☐ Sun

Hardiness Zone: _____

Soil Requirements: _____ Watering Requirements: _____

Season of Bloom: _____ Spacing: _____

Plant Width: _____ Plant Height: _____ Root Depth: _____

Care Notes (Pruning/Pest/Weed Control/Propagation/Fertilizer):

_____
_____
_____

Notes: _____
_____
_____
_____
_____

PLANT LOGBOOK

Plant Name (Common): _____

Genus Name: _____

☐ Bulb ☐ Herb ☐ Vegetable ☐ Shrub ☐ Tree ☐ Flower ☐ Indoor

☐ Rhizome ☐ Seedling ☐ Perennial ☐ Annual ☐ Biennial ☐ Outdoor

☐ Tuber ☐ Bare Root ☐ Vine ☐ Ornamental ☐ Fruit ☐ Groundcover

Attracts: _____

Resists: _____

Special Features: _____

Location Placed: _____

Date Planted: _____

Date Germinated: _____

Light Requirements:

☐ Shade ☐ Partial Sun ☐ Sun

Hardiness Zone: _____

Soil Requirements: _____ Watering Requirements: _____

Season of Bloom: _____ Spacing: _____

Plant Width: _____ Plant Height: _____ Root Depth: _____

Care Notes (Pruning/Pest/Weed Control/Propagation/Fertilizer):

_____

_____

_____

Notes: _____

_____

_____

_____

_____

PLANT LOGBOOK

Plant Name (Common): _____

Genus Name: _____

☐ Bulb ☐ Herb ☐ Vegetable ☐ Shrub ☐ Tree ☐ Flower ☐ Indoor

☐ Rhizome ☐ Seedling ☐ Perennial ☐ Annual ☐ Biennial ☐ Outdoor

☐ Tuber ☐ Bare Root ☐ Vine ☐ Ornamental ☐ Fruit ☐ Groundcover

Attracts: _____

Resists: _____

Special Features: _____

Location Placed: _____

Date Planted: _____

Date Germinated: _____

Light Requirements:

☐ Shade ☐ Partial Sun ☐ Sun

Hardiness Zone: _____

Soil Requirements: _____ Watering Requirements: _____

Season of Bloom: _____ Spacing: _____

Plant Width: _____ Plant Height: _____ Root Depth: _____

Care Notes (Pruning/Pest/Weed Control/Propagation/Fertilizer):

_____
_____
_____

Notes: _____
_____
_____
_____
_____

PLANT LOGBOOK

Plant Name (Common): _____

Genus Name: _____

☐ Bulb ☐ Herb ☐ Vegetable ☐ Shrub ☐ Tree ☐ Flower ☐ Indoor

☐ Rhizome ☐ Seedling ☐ Perennial ☐ Annual ☐ Biennial ☐ Outdoor

☐ Tuber ☐ Bare Root ☐ Vine ☐ Ornamental ☐ Fruit ☐ Groundcover

Attracts: _____

Resists: _____

Special Features: _____

Location Placed: _____

Date Planted: _____

Date Germinated: _____

Light Requirements:

☐ Shade ☐ Partial Sun ☐ Sun

Hardiness Zone: _____

Soil Requirements: _____ Watering Requirements: _____

Season of Bloom: _____ Spacing: _____

Plant Width: _____ Plant Height: _____ Root Depth: _____

Care Notes (Pruning/Pest/Weed Control/Propagation/Fertilizer):

_____
_____
_____

Notes: _____
_____
_____
_____
_____

PLANT LOGBOOK

Plant Name (Common): _____

Genus Name: _____

☐ Bulb ☐ Herb ☐ Vegetable ☐ Shrub ☐ Tree ☐ Flower ☐ Indoor

☐ Rhizome ☐ Seedling ☐ Perennial ☐ Annual ☐ Biennial ☐ Outdoor

☐ Tuber ☐ Bare Root ☐ Vine ☐ Ornamental ☐ Fruit ☐ Groundcover

Attracts: _____

Resists: _____

Special Features: _____

Location Placed: _____

Date Planted: _____

Date Germinated: _____

Light Requirements:

☐ Shade ☐ Partial Sun ☐ Sun

Hardiness Zone: _____

Soil Requirements: _____ Watering Requirements: _____

Season of Bloom: _____ Spacing: _____

Plant Width: _____ Plant Height: _____ Root Depth: _____

Care Notes (Pruning/Pest/Weed Control/Propagation/Fertilizer):
_____
_____
_____

Notes: _____
_____
_____
_____
_____

PLANT LOGBOOK

Plant Name (Common): _____

Genus Name: _____

☐ Bulb ☐ Herb ☐ Vegetable ☐ Shrub ☐ Tree ☐ Flower ☐ Indoor

☐ Rhizome ☐ Seedling ☐ Perennial ☐ Annual ☐ Biennial ☐ Outdoor

☐ Tuber ☐ Bare Root ☐ Vine ☐ Ornamental ☐ Fruit ☐ Groundcover

Attracts: _____

Resists: _____

Special Features: _____

Location Placed: _____

Date Planted: _____

Date Germinated: _____

Light Requirements:

☐ Shade ☐ Partial Sun ☐ Sun

Hardiness Zone: _____

Soil Requirements: _____ Watering Requirements: _____

Season of Bloom: _____ Spacing: _____

Plant Width: _____ Plant Height: _____ Root Depth: _____

Care Notes (Pruning/Pest/Weed Control/Propagation/Fertilizer):

_____
_____
_____
_____

Notes: _____
_____
_____
_____
_____
_____

PLANT LOGBOOK

Plant Name (Common): _____

Genus Name: _____

☐ Bulb ☐ Herb ☐ Vegetable ☐ Shrub ☐ Tree ☐ Flower ☐ Indoor

☐ Rhizome ☐ Seedling ☐ Perennial ☐ Annual ☐ Biennial ☐ Outdoor

☐ Tuber ☐ Bare Root ☐ Vine ☐ Ornamental ☐ Fruit ☐ Groundcover

Attracts: _____

Resists: _____

Special Features: _____

Location Placed: _____

Date Planted: _____

Date Germinated: _____

Light Requirements:

☐ Shade ☐ Partial Sun ☐ Sun

Hardiness Zone: _____

Soil Requirements: _____ Watering Requirements: _____

Season of Bloom: _____ Spacing: _____

Plant Width: _____ Plant Height: _____ Root Depth: _____

Care Notes (Pruning/Pest/Weed Control/Propagation/Fertilizer):

_____
_____
_____

Notes: _____
_____
_____
_____
_____

PLANT LOGBOOK

Plant Name (Common): _____

Genus Name: _____

☐ Bulb ☐ Herb ☐ Vegetable ☐ Shrub ☐ Tree ☐ Flower ☐ Indoor

☐ Rhizome ☐ Seedling ☐ Perennial ☐ Annual ☐ Biennial ☐ Outdoor

☐ Tuber ☐ Bare Root ☐ Vine ☐ Ornamental ☐ Fruit ☐ Groundcover

Attracts: _____

Resists: _____

Special Features: _____

Location Placed: _____

Date Planted: _____

Date Germinated: _____

Light Requirements:

☐ Shade ☐ Partial Sun ☐ Sun

Hardiness Zone: _____

Soil Requirements: _____ Watering Requirements: _____

Season of Bloom: _____ Spacing: _____

Plant Width: _____ Plant Height: _____ Root Depth: _____

Care Notes (Pruning/Pest/Weed Control/Propagation/Fertilizer):

_____
_____
_____

Notes: _____
_____
_____
_____
_____

PLANT LOGBOOK

Plant Name (Common): _____

Genus Name: _____

☐ Bulb ☐ Herb ☐ Vegetable ☐ Shrub ☐ Tree ☐ Flower ☐ Indoor

☐ Rhizome ☐ Seedling ☐ Perennial ☐ Annual ☐ Biennial ☐ Outdoor

☐ Tuber ☐ Bare Root ☐ Vine ☐ Ornamental ☐ Fruit ☐ Groundcover

Attracts: _____

Resists: _____

Special Features: _____

Location Placed: _____

Date Planted: _____

Date Germinated: _____

Light Requirements:

☐ Shade ☐ Partial Sun ☐ Sun

Hardiness Zone: _____

Soil Requirements: _____ Watering Requirements: _____

Season of Bloom: _____ Spacing: _____

Plant Width: _____ Plant Height: _____ Root Depth: _____

Care Notes (Pruning/Pest/Weed Control/Propagation/Fertilizer):

_____
_____
_____

Notes: _____
_____
_____
_____
_____

PLANT LOGBOOK

Plant Name (Common): _____

Genus Name: _____

☐ Bulb ☐ Herb ☐ Vegetable ☐ Shrub ☐ Tree ☐ Flower ☐ Indoor

☐ Rhizome ☐ Seedling ☐ Perennial ☐ Annual ☐ Biennial ☐ Outdoor

☐ Tuber ☐ Bare Root ☐ Vine ☐ Ornamental ☐ Fruit ☐ Groundcover

Attracts: _____

Resists: _____

Special Features: _____

Location Placed: _____

Date Planted: _____

Date Germinated: _____

Light Requirements:

☐ Shade ☐ Partial Sun ☐ Sun

Hardiness Zone: _____

Soil Requirements: _____ Watering Requirements: _____

Season of Bloom: _____ Spacing: _____

Plant Width: _____ Plant Height: _____ Root Depth: _____

Care Notes (Pruning/Pest/Weed Control/Propagation/Fertilizer):

_____

_____

_____

Notes: _____

_____

_____

_____

PLANT LOGBOOK

Plant Name (Common): _____

Genus Name: _____

☐ Bulb ☐ Herb ☐ Vegetable ☐ Shrub ☐ Tree ☐ Flower ☐ Indoor

☐ Rhizome ☐ Seedling ☐ Perennial ☐ Annual ☐ Biennial ☐ Outdoor

☐ Tuber ☐ Bare Root ☐ Vine ☐ Ornamental ☐ Fruit ☐ Groundcover

Attracts: _____

Resists: _____

Special Features: _____

Location Placed: _____

Date Planted: _____

Date Germinated: _____

Light Requirements:

☐ Shade ☐ Partial Sun ☐ Sun

Hardiness Zone: _____

Soil Requirements: _____ Watering Requirements: _____

Season of Bloom: _____ Spacing: _____

Plant Width: _____ Plant Height: _____ Root Depth: _____

Care Notes (Pruning/Pest/Weed Control/Propagation/Fertilizer):

_____

_____

_____

Notes: _____

_____

_____

_____

_____

PLANT LOGBOOK

Plant Name (Common): _____

Genus Name: _____

☐ Bulb ☐ Herb ☐ Vegetable ☐ Shrub ☐ Tree ☐ Flower ☐ Indoor

☐ Rhizome ☐ Seedling ☐ Perennial ☐ Annual ☐ Biennial ☐ Outdoor

☐ Tuber ☐ Bare Root ☐ Vine ☐ Ornamental ☐ Fruit ☐ Groundcover

Attracts: _____

Resists: _____

Special Features: _____

Location Placed: _____

Date Planted: _____

Date Germinated: _____

Light Requirements:

☐ Shade ☐ Partial Sun ☐ Sun

Hardiness Zone: _____

Soil Requirements: _____ Watering Requirements: _____

Season of Bloom: _____ Spacing: _____

Plant Width: _____ Plant Height: _____ Root Depth: _____

Care Notes (Pruning/Pest/Weed Control/Propagation/Fertilizer):

_____
_____
_____

Notes: _____
_____
_____
_____
_____

PLANT LOGBOOK

Plant Name (Common): _____

Genus Name: _____

☐ Bulb ☐ Herb ☐ Vegetable ☐ Shrub ☐ Tree ☐ Flower ☐ Indoor

☐ Rhizome ☐ Seedling ☐ Perennial ☐ Annual ☐ Biennial ☐ Outdoor

☐ Tuber ☐ Bare Root ☐ Vine ☐ Ornamental ☐ Fruit ☐ Groundcover

Attracts: _____

Resists: _____

Special Features: _____

Location Placed: _____

Date Planted: _____

Date Germinated: _____

Light Requirements:

☐ Shade ☐ Partial Sun ☐ Sun

Hardiness Zone: _____

Soil Requirements: _____ Watering Requirements: _____

Season of Bloom: _____ Spacing: _____

Plant Width: _____ Plant Height: _____ Root Depth: _____

Care Notes (Pruning/Pest/Weed Control/Propagation/Fertilizer):

_____

_____

_____

Notes: _____

_____

_____

_____

PLANT LOGBOOK

Plant Name (Common): _____

Genus Name: _____

☐ Bulb ☐ Herb ☐ Vegetable ☐ Shrub ☐ Tree ☐ Flower ☐ Indoor

☐ Rhizome ☐ Seedling ☐ Perennial ☐ Annual ☐ Biennial ☐ Outdoor

☐ Tuber ☐ Bare Root ☐ Vine ☐ Ornamental ☐ Fruit ☐ Groundcover

Attracts: _____

Resists: _____

Special Features: _____

Location Placed: _____

Date Planted: _____

Date Germinated: _____

Light Requirements:

☐ Shade ☐ Partial Sun ☐ Sun

Hardiness Zone: _____

Soil Requirements: _____ Watering Requirements: _____

Season of Bloom: _____ Spacing: _____

Plant Width: _____ Plant Height: _____ Root Depth: _____

Care Notes (Pruning/Pest/Weed Control/Propagation/Fertilizer):

_____
_____
_____
_____

Notes: _____
_____
_____
_____
_____

PLANT LOGBOOK

Plant Name (Common): _____

Genus Name: _____

☐ Bulb ☐ Herb ☐ Vegetable ☐ Shrub ☐ Tree ☐ Flower ☐ Indoor

☐ Rhizome ☐ Seedling ☐ Perennial ☐ Annual ☐ Biennial ☐ Outdoor

☐ Tuber ☐ Bare Root ☐ Vine ☐ Ornamental ☐ Fruit ☐ Groundcover

Attracts: _____

Resists: _____

Special Features: _____

Location Placed: _____

Date Planted: _____

Date Germinated: _____

Light Requirements:

☐ Shade   ☐ Partial Sun   ☐ Sun

Hardiness Zone: _____

Soil Requirements: _____   Watering Requirements: _____

Season of Bloom: _____   Spacing: _____

Plant Width: _____   Plant Height: _____   Root Depth: _____

Care Notes (Pruning/Pest/Weed Control/Propagation/Fertilizer):

_____
_____
_____

Notes: _____

_____
_____
_____
_____

PLANT LOGBOOK

Plant Name (Common): _____

Genus Name: _____

☐ Bulb ☐ Herb ☐ Vegetable ☐ Shrub ☐ Tree ☐ Flower ☐ Indoor

☐ Rhizome ☐ Seedling ☐ Perennial ☐ Annual ☐ Biennial ☐ Outdoor

☐ Tuber ☐ Bare Root ☐ Vine ☐ Ornamental ☐ Fruit ☐ Groundcover

Attracts: _____

Resists: _____

Special Features: _____

Location Placed: _____

Date Planted: _____

Date Germinated: _____

Light Requirements:

☐ Shade ☐ Partial Sun ☐ Sun

Hardiness Zone: _____

Soil Requirements: _____ Watering Requirements: _____

Season of Bloom: _____ Spacing: _____

Plant Width: _____ Plant Height: _____ Root Depth: _____

Care Notes (Pruning/Pest/Weed Control/Propagation/Fertilizer):

_____
_____
_____

Notes: _____
_____
_____
_____
_____

PLANT LOGBOOK

Plant Name (Common): _____

Genus Name: _____

☐ Bulb   ☐ Herb   ☐ Vegetable   ☐ Shrub   ☐ Tree   ☐ Flower   ☐ Indoor

☐ Rhizome   ☐ Seedling   ☐ Perennial   ☐ Annual   ☐ Biennial   ☐ Outdoor

☐ Tuber   ☐ Bare Root   ☐ Vine   ☐ Ornamental   ☐ Fruit   ☐ Groundcover

Attracts: _____

Resists: _____

Special Features: _____

Location Placed: _____

Date Planted: _____

Date Germinated: _____

Light Requirements:

☐ Shade   ☐ Partial Sun   ☐ Sun

Hardiness Zone: _____

Soil Requirements: _____   Watering Requirements: _____

Season of Bloom: _____   Spacing: _____

Plant Width: _____   Plant Height: _____   Root Depth: _____

Care Notes (Pruning/Pest/Weed Control/Propagation/Fertilizer):

_____
_____
_____

Notes: _____
_____
_____
_____
_____

PLANT LOGBOOK

Plant Name (Common): _____

Genus Name: _____

☐ Bulb ☐ Herb ☐ Vegetable ☐ Shrub ☐ Tree ☐ Flower ☐ Indoor

☐ Rhizome ☐ Seedling ☐ Perennial ☐ Annual ☐ Biennial ☐ Outdoor

☐ Tuber ☐ Bare Root ☐ Vine ☐ Ornamental ☐ Fruit ☐ Groundcover

Attracts: _____

Resists: _____

Special Features: _____

Location Placed: _____

Date Planted: _____

Date Germinated: _____

Light Requirements:

☐ Shade ☐ Partial Sun ☐ Sun

Hardiness Zone: _____

Soil Requirements: _____ Watering Requirements: _____

Season of Bloom: _____ Spacing: _____

Plant Width: _____ Plant Height: _____ Root Depth: _____

Care Notes (Pruning/Pest/Weed Control/Propagation/Fertilizer):

_____
_____
_____

Notes: _____
_____
_____
_____
_____
_____

PLANT LOGBOOK

Plant Name (Common): _____

Genus Name: _____

☐ Bulb ☐ Herb ☐ Vegetable ☐ Shrub ☐ Tree ☐ Flower ☐ Indoor

☐ Rhizome ☐ Seedling ☐ Perennial ☐ Annual ☐ Biennial ☐ Outdoor

☐ Tuber ☐ Bare Root ☐ Vine ☐ Ornamental ☐ Fruit ☐ Groundcover

Attracts: _____

Resists: _____

Special Features: _____

Location Placed: _____

Date Planted: _____

Date Germinated: _____

Light Requirements:

☐ Shade ☐ Partial Sun ☐ Sun

Hardiness Zone: _____

Soil Requirements: _____ Watering Requirements: _____

Season of Bloom: _____ Spacing: _____

Plant Width: _____ Plant Height: _____ Root Depth: _____

Care Notes (Pruning/Pest/Weed Control/Propagation/Fertilizer):

_____
_____
_____

Notes: _____
_____
_____
_____
_____

PLANT LOGBOOK

Plant Name (Common): _____

Genus Name: _____

☐ Bulb ☐ Herb ☐ Vegetable ☐ Shrub ☐ Tree ☐ Flower ☐ Indoor

☐ Rhizome ☐ Seedling ☐ Perennial ☐ Annual ☐ Biennial ☐ Outdoor

☐ Tuber ☐ Bare Root ☐ Vine ☐ Ornamental ☐ Fruit ☐ Groundcover

Attracts: _____

Resists: _____

Special Features: _____

Location Placed: _____

Date Planted: _____

Date Germinated: _____

Light Requirements:

☐ Shade ☐ Partial Sun ☐ Sun

Hardiness Zone: _____

Soil Requirements: _____ Watering Requirements: _____

Season of Bloom: _____ Spacing: _____

Plant Width: _____ Plant Height: _____ Root Depth: _____

Care Notes (Pruning/Pest/Weed Control/Propagation/Fertilizer):

_____
_____
_____

Notes: _____
_____
_____
_____
_____

PLANT LOGBOOK

Plant Name (Common): _____

Genus Name: _____

☐ Bulb ☐ Herb ☐ Vegetable ☐ Shrub ☐ Tree ☐ Flower ☐ Indoor

☐ Rhizome ☐ Seedling ☐ Perennial ☐ Annual ☐ Biennial ☐ Outdoor

☐ Tuber ☐ Bare Root ☐ Vine ☐ Ornamental ☐ Fruit ☐ Groundcover

Attracts: _____

Resists: _____

Special Features: _____

Location Placed: _____

Date Planted: _____

Date Germinated: _____

Light Requirements:

☐ Shade ☐ Partial Sun ☐ Sun

Hardiness Zone: _____

Soil Requirements: _____ Watering Requirements: _____

Season of Bloom: _____ Spacing: _____

Plant Width: _____ Plant Height: _____ Root Depth: _____

Care Notes (Pruning/Pest/Weed Control/Propagation/Fertilizer):

_____
_____
_____

Notes: _____
_____
_____
_____
_____

PLANT LOGBOOK

Plant Name (Common): _____

Genus Name: _____

☐ Bulb ☐ Herb ☐ Vegetable ☐ Shrub ☐ Tree ☐ Flower ☐ Indoor

☐ Rhizome ☐ Seedling ☐ Perennial ☐ Annual ☐ Biennial ☐ Outdoor

☐ Tuber ☐ Bare Root ☐ Vine ☐ Ornamental ☐ Fruit ☐ Groundcover

Attracts: _____

Resists: _____

Special Features: _____

Location Placed: _____

Date Planted: _____

Date Germinated: _____

Light Requirements:

☐ Shade ☐ Partial Sun ☐ Sun

Hardiness Zone: _____

Soil Requirements: _____ Watering Requirements: _____

Season of Bloom: _____ Spacing: _____

Plant Width: _____ Plant Height: _____ Root Depth: _____

Care Notes (Pruning/Pest/Weed Control/Propagation/Fertilizer):

_____
_____
_____

Notes: _____
_____
_____
_____
_____

PLANT LOGBOOK

Plant Name (Common): _____

Genus Name: _____

☐ Bulb ☐ Herb ☐ Vegetable ☐ Shrub ☐ Tree ☐ Flower ☐ Indoor

☐ Rhizome ☐ Seedling ☐ Perennial ☐ Annual ☐ Biennial ☐ Outdoor

☐ Tuber ☐ Bare Root ☐ Vine ☐ Ornamental ☐ Fruit ☐ Groundcover

Attracts: _____

Resists: _____

Special Features: _____

Location Placed: _____

Date Planted: _____

Date Germinated: _____

Light Requirements:

☐ Shade ☐ Partial Sun ☐ Sun

Hardiness Zone: _____

Soil Requirements: _____ Watering Requirements: _____

Season of Bloom: _____ Spacing: _____

Plant Width: _____ Plant Height: _____ Root Depth: _____

Care Notes (Pruning/Pest/Weed Control/Propagation/Fertilizer):

_____
_____
_____

Notes: _____
_____
_____
_____
_____

PLANT LOGBOOK

Plant Name (Common): _____

Genus Name: _____

☐ Bulb ☐ Herb ☐ Vegetable ☐ Shrub ☐ Tree ☐ Flower ☐ Indoor

☐ Rhizome ☐ Seedling ☐ Perennial ☐ Annual ☐ Biennial ☐ Outdoor

☐ Tuber ☐ Bare Root ☐ Vine ☐ Ornamental ☐ Fruit ☐ Groundcover

Attracts: _____

Resists: _____

Special Features: _____

Location Placed: _____

Date Planted: _____

Date Germinated: _____

Light Requirements:

☐ Shade ☐ Partial Sun ☐ Sun

Hardiness Zone: _____

Soil Requirements: _____ Watering Requirements: _____

Season of Bloom: _____ Spacing: _____

Plant Width: _____ Plant Height: _____ Root Depth: _____

Care Notes (Pruning/Pest/Weed Control/Propagation/Fertilizer):

_____
_____
_____

Notes: _____
_____
_____
_____
_____

PLANT LOGBOOK

Plant Name (Common): _____

Genus Name: _____

☐ Bulb ☐ Herb ☐ Vegetable ☐ Shrub ☐ Tree ☐ Flower ☐ Indoor

☐ Rhizome ☐ Seedling ☐ Perennial ☐ Annual ☐ Biennial ☐ Outdoor

☐ Tuber ☐ Bare Root ☐ Vine ☐ Ornamental ☐ Fruit ☐ Groundcover

Attracts: _____

Resists: _____

Special Features: _____

Location Placed: _____

Date Planted: _____

Date Germinated: _____

Light Requirements:

☐ Shade ☐ Partial Sun ☐ Sun

Hardiness Zone: _____

Soil Requirements: _____ Watering Requirements: _____

Season of Bloom: _____ Spacing: _____

Plant Width: _____ Plant Height: _____ Root Depth: _____

Care Notes (Pruning/Pest/Weed Control/Propagation/Fertilizer):

_____
_____
_____

Notes: _____
_____
_____
_____
_____

PLANT LOGBOOK

Plant Name (Common): _____

Genus Name: _____

☐ Bulb ☐ Herb ☐ Vegetable ☐ Shrub ☐ Tree ☐ Flower ☐ Indoor

☐ Rhizome ☐ Seedling ☐ Perennial ☐ Annual ☐ Biennial ☐ Outdoor

☐ Tuber ☐ Bare Root ☐ Vine ☐ Ornamental ☐ Fruit ☐ Groundcover

Attracts: _____

Resists: _____

Special Features: _____

Location Placed: _____

Date Planted: _____

Date Germinated: _____

Light Requirements:

☐ Shade ☐ Partial Sun ☐ Sun

Hardiness Zone: _____

Soil Requirements: _____ Watering Requirements: _____

Season of Bloom: _____ Spacing: _____

Plant Width: _____ Plant Height: _____ Root Depth: _____

Care Notes (Pruning/Pest/Weed Control/Propagation/Fertilizer):

_____
_____
_____
_____

Notes: _____
_____
_____
_____
_____

PLANT LOGBOOK

Plant Name (Common): _____

Genus Name: _____

☐ Bulb ☐ Herb ☐ Vegetable ☐ Shrub ☐ Tree ☐ Flower ☐ Indoor

☐ Rhizome ☐ Seedling ☐ Perennial ☐ Annual ☐ Biennial ☐ Outdoor

☐ Tuber ☐ Bare Root ☐ Vine ☐ Ornamental ☐ Fruit ☐ Groundcover

Attracts: _____

Resists: _____

Special Features: _____

Location Placed: _____

Date Planted: _____

Date Germinated: _____

Light Requirements:

☐ Shade ☐ Partial Sun ☐ Sun

Hardiness Zone: _____

Soil Requirements: _____ Watering Requirements: _____

Season of Bloom: _____ Spacing: _____

Plant Width: _____ Plant Height: _____ Root Depth: _____

Care Notes (Pruning/Pest/Weed Control/Propagation/Fertilizer):

_____

_____

_____

Notes: _____

_____

_____

_____

PLANT LOGBOOK

Plant Name (Common): _____

Genus Name: _____

☐ Bulb ☐ Herb ☐ Vegetable ☐ Shrub ☐ Tree ☐ Flower ☐ Indoor

☐ Rhizome ☐ Seedling ☐ Perennial ☐ Annual ☐ Biennial ☐ Outdoor

☐ Tuber ☐ Bare Root ☐ Vine ☐ Ornamental ☐ Fruit ☐ Groundcover

Attracts: _____

Resists: _____

Special Features: _____

Location Placed: _____

Date Planted: _____

Date Germinated: _____

Light Requirements:

☐ Shade ☐ Partial Sun ☐ Sun

Hardiness Zone: _____

Soil Requirements: _____ Watering Requirements: _____

Season of Bloom: _____ Spacing: _____

Plant Width: _____ Plant Height: _____ Root Depth: _____

Care Notes (Pruning/Pest/Weed Control/Propagation/Fertilizer):

_____
_____
_____

Notes: _____
_____
_____
_____
_____

PLANT LOGBOOK

Plant Name (Common): _____

Genus Name: _____

☐ Bulb ☐ Herb ☐ Vegetable ☐ Shrub ☐ Tree ☐ Flower ☐ Indoor

☐ Rhizome ☐ Seedling ☐ Perennial ☐ Annual ☐ Biennial ☐ Outdoor

☐ Tuber ☐ Bare Root ☐ Vine ☐ Ornamental ☐ Fruit ☐ Groundcover

Attracts: _____

Resists: _____

Special Features: _____

Location Placed: _____

Date Planted: _____

Date Germinated: _____

Light Requirements:

☐ Shade ☐ Partial Sun ☐ Sun

Hardiness Zone: _____

Soil Requirements: _____ Watering Requirements: _____

Season of Bloom: _____ Spacing: _____

Plant Width: _____ Plant Height: _____ Root Depth: _____

Care Notes (Pruning/Pest/Weed Control/Propagation/Fertilizer):

_____

_____

_____

Notes: _____

_____

_____

_____

_____

PLANT LOGBOOK

Plant Name (Common): _____

Genus Name: _____

☐ Bulb ☐ Herb ☐ Vegetable ☐ Shrub ☐ Tree ☐ Flower ☐ Indoor

☐ Rhizome ☐ Seedling ☐ Perennial ☐ Annual ☐ Biennial ☐ Outdoor

☐ Tuber ☐ Bare Root ☐ Vine ☐ Ornamental ☐ Fruit ☐ Groundcover

Attracts: _____

Resists: _____

Special Features: _____

Location Placed: _____

Date Planted: _____

Date Germinated: _____

Light Requirements:

☐ Shade ☐ Partial Sun ☐ Sun

Hardiness Zone: _____

Soil Requirements: _____ Watering Requirements: _____

Season of Bloom: _____ Spacing: _____

Plant Width: _____ Plant Height: _____ Root Depth: _____

Care Notes (Pruning/Pest/Weed Control/Propagation/Fertilizer):

_____
_____
_____
_____

Notes: _____
_____
_____
_____
_____

PLANT LOGBOOK

Plant Name (Common): _____

Genus Name: _____

☐ Bulb ☐ Herb ☐ Vegetable ☐ Shrub ☐ Tree ☐ Flower ☐ Indoor

☐ Rhizome ☐ Seedling ☐ Perennial ☐ Annual ☐ Biennial ☐ Outdoor

☐ Tuber ☐ Bare Root ☐ Vine ☐ Ornamental ☐ Fruit ☐ Groundcover

Attracts: _____

Resists: _____

Special Features: _____

Location Placed: _____

Date Planted: _____

Date Germinated: _____

Light Requirements:

☐ Shade ☐ Partial Sun ☐ Sun

Hardiness Zone: _____

Soil Requirements: _____ Watering Requirements: _____

Season of Bloom: _____ Spacing: _____

Plant Width: _____ Plant Height: _____ Root Depth: _____

Care Notes (Pruning/Pest/Weed Control/Propagation/Fertilizer):

_____

_____

_____

Notes: _____

_____

_____

_____

_____

PLANT LOGBOOK

Plant Name (Common): _____

Genus Name: _____

☐ Bulb ☐ Herb ☐ Vegetable ☐ Shrub ☐ Tree ☐ Flower ☐ Indoor

☐ Rhizome ☐ Seedling ☐ Perennial ☐ Annual ☐ Biennial ☐ Outdoor

☐ Tuber ☐ Bare Root ☐ Vine ☐ Ornamental ☐ Fruit ☐ Groundcover

Attracts: _____

Resists: _____

Special Features: _____

Location Placed: _____

Date Planted: _____

Date Germinated: _____

Light Requirements:

☐ Shade ☐ Partial Sun ☐ Sun

Hardiness Zone: _____

Soil Requirements: _____ Watering Requirements: _____

Season of Bloom: _____ Spacing: _____

Plant Width: _____ Plant Height: _____ Root Depth: _____

Care Notes (Pruning/Pest/Weed Control/Propagation/Fertilizer):

_____

_____

_____

Notes: _____

_____

_____

_____

_____

PLANT LOGBOOK

Plant Name (Common): _____

Genus Name: _____

☐ Bulb ☐ Herb ☐ Vegetable ☐ Shrub ☐ Tree ☐ Flower ☐ Indoor

☐ Rhizome ☐ Seedling ☐ Perennial ☐ Annual ☐ Biennial ☐ Outdoor

☐ Tuber ☐ Bare Root ☐ Vine ☐ Ornamental ☐ Fruit ☐ Groundcover

Attracts: _____

Resists: _____

Special Features: _____

Location Placed: _____

Date Planted: _____

Date Germinated: _____

Light Requirements:

☐ Shade ☐ Partial Sun ☐ Sun

Hardiness Zone: _____

Soil Requirements: _____ Watering Requirements: _____

Season of Bloom: _____ Spacing: _____

Plant Width: _____ Plant Height: _____ Root Depth: _____

Care Notes (Pruning/Pest/Weed Control/Propagation/Fertilizer):

_____
_____
_____

Notes: _____
_____
_____
_____
_____

PLANT LOGBOOK

Plant Name (Common): _____

Genus Name: _____

☐ Bulb ☐ Herb ☐ Vegetable ☐ Shrub ☐ Tree ☐ Flower ☐ Indoor

☐ Rhizome ☐ Seedling ☐ Perennial ☐ Annual ☐ Biennial ☐ Outdoor

☐ Tuber ☐ Bare Root ☐ Vine ☐ Ornamental ☐ Fruit ☐ Groundcover

Attracts: _____

Resists: _____

Special Features: _____

Location Placed: _____

Date Planted: _____

Date Germinated: _____

Light Requirements:

☐ Shade ☐ Partial Sun ☐ Sun

Hardiness Zone: _____

Soil Requirements: _____ Watering Requirements: _____

Season of Bloom: _____ Spacing: _____

Plant Width: _____ Plant Height: _____ Root Depth: _____

Care Notes (Pruning/Pest/Weed Control/Propagation/Fertilizer):

_____
_____
_____
_____

Notes: _____
_____
_____
_____
_____

PLANT LOGBOOK

Plant Name (Common): _____

Genus Name: _____

☐ Bulb ☐ Herb ☐ Vegetable ☐ Shrub ☐ Tree ☐ Flower ☐ Indoor

☐ Rhizome ☐ Seedling ☐ Perennial ☐ Annual ☐ Biennial ☐ Outdoor

☐ Tuber ☐ Bare Root ☐ Vine ☐ Ornamental ☐ Fruit ☐ Groundcover

Attracts: _____

Resists: _____

Special Features: _____

Location Placed: _____

Date Planted: _____

Date Germinated: _____

Light Requirements:

☐ Shade ☐ Partial Sun ☐ Sun

Hardiness Zone: _____

Soil Requirements: _____ Watering Requirements: _____

Season of Bloom: _____ Spacing: _____

Plant Width: _____ Plant Height: _____ Root Depth: _____

Care Notes (Pruning/Pest/Weed Control/Propagation/Fertilizer):

_____
_____
_____

Notes: _____
_____
_____
_____
_____

PLANT LOGBOOK

Plant Name (Common): _____

Genus Name: _____

☐ Bulb ☐ Herb ☐ Vegetable ☐ Shrub ☐ Tree ☐ Flower ☐ Indoor

☐ Rhizome ☐ Seedling ☐ Perennial ☐ Annual ☐ Biennial ☐ Outdoor

☐ Tuber ☐ Bare Root ☐ Vine ☐ Ornamental ☐ Fruit ☐ Groundcover

Attracts: _____

Resists: _____

Special Features: _____

Location Placed: _____

Date Planted: _____

Date Germinated: _____

Light Requirements:

☐ Shade ☐ Partial Sun ☐ Sun

Hardiness Zone: _____

Soil Requirements: _____ Watering Requirements: _____

Season of Bloom: _____ Spacing: _____

Plant Width: _____ Plant Height: _____ Root Depth: _____

Care Notes (Pruning/Pest/Weed Control/Propagation/Fertilizer):

_____

_____

_____

Notes: _____

_____

_____

_____

_____

PLANT LOGBOOK

Plant Name (Common): _____

Genus Name: _____

☐ Bulb ☐ Herb ☐ Vegetable ☐ Shrub ☐ Tree ☐ Flower ☐ Indoor

☐ Rhizome ☐ Seedling ☐ Perennial ☐ Annual ☐ Biennial ☐ Outdoor

☐ Tuber ☐ Bare Root ☐ Vine ☐ Ornamental ☐ Fruit ☐ Groundcover

Attracts: _____

Resists: _____

Special Features: _____

Location Placed: _____

Date Planted: _____

Date Germinated: _____

Light Requirements:

☐ Shade ☐ Partial Sun ☐ Sun

Hardiness Zone: _____

Soil Requirements: _____ Watering Requirements: _____

Season of Bloom: _____ Spacing: _____

Plant Width: _____ Plant Height: _____ Root Depth: _____

Care Notes (Pruning/Pest/Weed Control/Propagation/Fertilizer):

_____

_____

_____

Notes: _____

_____

_____

_____

_____

PLANT LOGBOOK

Plant Name (Common): _____

Genus Name: _____

☐ Bulb ☐ Herb ☐ Vegetable ☐ Shrub ☐ Tree ☐ Flower ☐ Indoor

☐ Rhizome ☐ Seedling ☐ Perennial ☐ Annual ☐ Biennial ☐ Outdoor

☐ Tuber ☐ Bare Root ☐ Vine ☐ Ornamental ☐ Fruit ☐ Groundcover

Attracts: _____

Resists: _____

Special Features: _____

Location Placed: _____

Date Planted: _____

Date Germinated: _____

Light Requirements:

☐ Shade ☐ Partial Sun ☐ Sun

Hardiness Zone: _____

Soil Requirements: _____ Watering Requirements: _____

Season of Bloom: _____ Spacing: _____

Plant Width: _____ Plant Height: _____ Root Depth: _____

Care Notes (Pruning/Pest/Weed Control/Propagation/Fertilizer):

_____

_____

_____

Notes: _____

_____

_____

_____

PLANT LOGBOOK

Plant Name (Common): _____

Genus Name: _____

☐ Bulb ☐ Herb ☐ Vegetable ☐ Shrub ☐ Tree ☐ Flower ☐ Indoor

☐ Rhizome ☐ Seedling ☐ Perennial ☐ Annual ☐ Biennial ☐ Outdoor

☐ Tuber ☐ Bare Root ☐ Vine ☐ Ornamental ☐ Fruit ☐ Groundcover

Attracts: _____

Resists: _____

Special Features: _____

Location Placed: _____

Date Planted: _____

Date Germinated: _____

Light Requirements:

☐ Shade ☐ Partial Sun ☐ Sun

Hardiness Zone: _____

Soil Requirements: _____ Watering Requirements: _____

Season of Bloom: _____ Spacing: _____

Plant Width: _____ Plant Height: _____ Root Depth: _____

Care Notes (Pruning/Pest/Weed Control/Propagation/Fertilizer):

_____

_____

_____

Notes: _____

_____

_____

_____

_____

PLANT LOGBOOK

Plant Name (Common): _____

Genus Name: _____

☐ Bulb ☐ Herb ☐ Vegetable ☐ Shrub ☐ Tree ☐ Flower ☐ Indoor

☐ Rhizome ☐ Seedling ☐ Perennial ☐ Annual ☐ Biennial ☐ Outdoor

☐ Tuber ☐ Bare Root ☐ Vine ☐ Ornamental ☐ Fruit ☐ Groundcover

Attracts: _____

Resists: _____

Special Features: _____

Location Placed: _____

Date Planted: _____

Date Germinated: _____

Light Requirements:

☐ Shade ☐ Partial Sun ☐ Sun

Hardiness Zone: _____

Soil Requirements: _____ Watering Requirements: _____

Season of Bloom: _____ Spacing: _____

Plant Width: _____ Plant Height: _____ Root Depth: _____

Care Notes (Pruning/Pest/Weed Control/Propagation/Fertilizer):

_____

_____

_____

Notes: _____

_____

_____

_____

_____

PLANT LOGBOOK

Plant Name (Common): _____

Genus Name: _____

☐ Bulb ☐ Herb ☐ Vegetable ☐ Shrub ☐ Tree ☐ Flower ☐ Indoor

☐ Rhizome ☐ Seedling ☐ Perennial ☐ Annual ☐ Biennial ☐ Outdoor

☐ Tuber ☐ Bare Root ☐ Vine ☐ Ornamental ☐ Fruit ☐ Groundcover

Attracts: _____

Resists: _____

Special Features: _____

Location Placed: _____

Date Planted: _____

Date Germinated: _____

Light Requirements:

☐ Shade ☐ Partial Sun ☐ Sun

Hardiness Zone: _____

Soil Requirements: _____ Watering Requirements: _____

Season of Bloom: _____ Spacing: _____

Plant Width: _____ Plant Height: _____ Root Depth: _____

Care Notes (Pruning/Pest/Weed Control/Propagation/Fertilizer):

_____
_____
_____

Notes: _____
_____
_____
_____
_____

PLANT LOGBOOK

Plant Name (Common): _____

Genus Name: _____

☐ Bulb ☐ Herb ☐ Vegetable ☐ Shrub ☐ Tree ☐ Flower ☐ Indoor

☐ Rhizome ☐ Seedling ☐ Perennial ☐ Annual ☐ Biennial ☐ Outdoor

☐ Tuber ☐ Bare Root ☐ Vine ☐ Ornamental ☐ Fruit ☐ Groundcover

Attracts: _____

Resists: _____

Special Features: _____

Location Placed: _____

Date Planted: _____

Date Germinated: _____

Light Requirements:

☐ Shade ☐ Partial Sun ☐ Sun

Hardiness Zone: _____

Soil Requirements: _____ Watering Requirements: _____

Season of Bloom: _____ Spacing: _____

Plant Width: _____ Plant Height: _____ Root Depth: _____

Care Notes (Pruning/Pest/Weed Control/Propagation/Fertilizer):

_____
_____
_____

Notes: _____
_____
_____
_____
_____

PLANT LOGBOOK

Plant Name (Common): _____

Genus Name: _____

☐ Bulb ☐ Herb ☐ Vegetable ☐ Shrub ☐ Tree ☐ Flower ☐ Indoor

☐ Rhizome ☐ Seedling ☐ Perennial ☐ Annual ☐ Biennial ☐ Outdoor

☐ Tuber ☐ Bare Root ☐ Vine ☐ Ornamental ☐ Fruit ☐ Groundcover

Attracts: _____

Resists: _____

Special Features: _____

Location Placed: _____

Date Planted: _____

Date Germinated: _____

Light Requirements:

☐ Shade ☐ Partial Sun ☐ Sun

Hardiness Zone: _____

Soil Requirements: _____ Watering Requirements: _____

Season of Bloom: _____ Spacing: _____

Plant Width: _____ Plant Height: _____ Root Depth: _____

Care Notes (Pruning/Pest/Weed Control/Propagation/Fertilizer):

_____

_____

_____

Notes: _____

_____

_____

_____

_____

PLANT LOGBOOK

Plant Name (Common): _____

Genus Name: _____

☐ Bulb ☐ Herb ☐ Vegetable ☐ Shrub ☐ Tree ☐ Flower ☐ Indoor

☐ Rhizome ☐ Seedling ☐ Perennial ☐ Annual ☐ Biennial ☐ Outdoor

☐ Tuber ☐ Bare Root ☐ Vine ☐ Ornamental ☐ Fruit ☐ Groundcover

Attracts: _____

Resists: _____

Special Features: _____

Location Placed: _____

Date Planted: _____

Date Germinated: _____

Light Requirements:

☐ Shade ☐ Partial Sun ☐ Sun

Hardiness Zone: _____

Soil Requirements: _____ Watering Requirements: _____

Season of Bloom: _____ Spacing: _____

Plant Width: _____ Plant Height: _____ Root Depth: _____

Care Notes (Pruning/Pest/Weed Control/Propagation/Fertilizer):

_____
_____
_____

Notes: _____
_____
_____
_____
_____

PLANT LOGBOOK

Plant Name (Common): _____

Genus Name: _____

☐ Bulb ☐ Herb ☐ Vegetable ☐ Shrub ☐ Tree ☐ Flower ☐ Indoor

☐ Rhizome ☐ Seedling ☐ Perennial ☐ Annual ☐ Biennial ☐ Outdoor

☐ Tuber ☐ Bare Root ☐ Vine ☐ Ornamental ☐ Fruit ☐ Groundcover

Attracts: _____

Resists: _____

Special Features: _____

Location Placed: _____

Date Planted: _____

Date Germinated: _____

Light Requirements:

☐ Shade ☐ Partial Sun ☐ Sun

Hardiness Zone: _____

Soil Requirements: _____ Watering Requirements: _____

Season of Bloom: _____ Spacing: _____

Plant Width: _____ Plant Height: _____ Root Depth: _____

Care Notes (Pruning/Pest/Weed Control/Propagation/Fertilizer):

_____
_____
_____

Notes: _____
_____
_____
_____

PLANT LOGBOOK

Plant Name (Common): _____

Genus Name: _____

☐ Bulb ☐ Herb ☐ Vegetable ☐ Shrub ☐ Tree ☐ Flower ☐ Indoor

☐ Rhizome ☐ Seedling ☐ Perennial ☐ Annual ☐ Biennial ☐ Outdoor

☐ Tuber ☐ Bare Root ☐ Vine ☐ Ornamental ☐ Fruit ☐ Groundcover

Attracts: _____

Resists: _____

Special Features: _____

Location Placed: _____

Date Planted: _____

Date Germinated: _____

Light Requirements:

☐ Shade ☐ Partial Sun ☐ Sun

Hardiness Zone: _____

Soil Requirements: _____ Watering Requirements: _____

Season of Bloom: _____ Spacing: _____

Plant Width: _____ Plant Height: _____ Root Depth: _____

Care Notes (Pruning/Pest/Weed Control/Propagation/Fertilizer):

_____
_____
_____
_____

Notes: _____
_____
_____
_____
_____

PLANT LOGBOOK

Plant Name (Common): _____

Genus Name: _____

☐ Bulb ☐ Herb ☐ Vegetable ☐ Shrub ☐Tree ☐ Flower ☐ Indoor

☐ Rhizome ☐ Seedling ☐ Perennial ☐ Annual ☐ Biennial ☐ Outdoor

☐ Tuber ☐ Bare Root ☐ Vine ☐ Ornamental ☐ Fruit ☐ Groundcover

Attracts: _____

Resists: _____

Special Features: _____

Location Placed: _____

Date Planted: _____

Date Germinated: _____

Light Requirements:

☐ Shade ☐ Partial Sun ☐ Sun

Hardiness Zone: _____

Soil Requirements: _____ Watering Requirements: _____

Season of Bloom: _____ Spacing: _____

Plant Width: _____ Plant Height: _____ Root Depth: _____

Care Notes (Pruning/Pest/Weed Control/Propagation/Fertilizer):

_____

_____

_____

Notes: _____

_____

_____

_____

_____

PLANT LOGBOOK

Plant Name (Common): _____

Genus Name: _____

☐ Bulb ☐ Herb ☐ Vegetable ☐ Shrub ☐ Tree ☐ Flower ☐ Indoor

☐ Rhizome ☐ Seedling ☐ Perennial ☐ Annual ☐ Biennial ☐ Outdoor

☐ Tuber ☐ Bare Root ☐ Vine ☐ Ornamental ☐ Fruit ☐ Groundcover

Attracts: _____

Resists: _____

Special Features: _____

Location Placed: _____

Date Planted: _____

Date Germinated: _____

Light Requirements:

☐ Shade ☐ Partial Sun ☐ Sun

Hardiness Zone: _____

Soil Requirements: _____ Watering Requirements: _____

Season of Bloom: _____ Spacing: _____

Plant Width: _____ Plant Height: _____ Root Depth: _____

Care Notes (Pruning/Pest/Weed Control/Propagation/Fertilizer):

_____
_____
_____

Notes: _____
_____
_____
_____
_____

PLANT LOGBOOK

Plant Name (Common): _____

Genus Name: _____

☐ Bulb ☐ Herb ☐ Vegetable ☐ Shrub ☐ Tree ☐ Flower ☐ Indoor

☐ Rhizome ☐ Seedling ☐ Perennial ☐ Annual ☐ Biennial ☐ Outdoor

☐ Tuber ☐ Bare Root ☐ Vine ☐ Ornamental ☐ Fruit ☐ Groundcover

Attracts: _____

Resists: _____

Special Features: _____

Location Placed: _____

Date Planted: _____

Date Germinated: _____

Light Requirements:

☐ Shade ☐ Partial Sun ☐ Sun

Hardiness Zone: _____

Soil Requirements: _____ Watering Requirements: _____

Season of Bloom: _____ Spacing: _____

Plant Width: _____ Plant Height: _____ Root Depth: _____

Care Notes (Pruning/Pest/Weed Control/Propagation/Fertilizer):

_____
_____
_____

Notes: _____
_____
_____
_____
_____

PLANT LOGBOOK

Plant Name (Common): _____

Genus Name: _____

☐ Bulb ☐ Herb ☐ Vegetable ☐ Shrub ☐ Tree ☐ Flower ☐ Indoor

☐ Rhizome ☐ Seedling ☐ Perennial ☐ Annual ☐ Biennial ☐ Outdoor

☐ Tuber ☐ Bare Root ☐ Vine ☐ Ornamental ☐ Fruit ☐ Groundcover

Attracts: _____

Resists: _____

Special Features: _____

Location Placed: _____

Date Planted: _____

Date Germinated: _____

Light Requirements:

☐ Shade ☐ Partial Sun ☐ Sun

Hardiness Zone: _____

Soil Requirements: _____ Watering Requirements: _____

Season of Bloom: _____ Spacing: _____

Plant Width: _____ Plant Height: _____ Root Depth: _____

Care Notes (Pruning/Pest/Weed Control/Propagation/Fertilizer):

_____
_____
_____
_____

Notes: _____
_____
_____
_____
_____

PLANT LOGBOOK

Plant Name (Common): _____

Genus Name: _____

☐ Bulb ☐ Herb ☐ Vegetable ☐ Shrub ☐ Tree ☐ Flower ☐ Indoor

☐ Rhizome ☐ Seedling ☐ Perennial ☐ Annual ☐ Biennial ☐ Outdoor

☐ Tuber ☐ Bare Root ☐ Vine ☐ Ornamental ☐ Fruit ☐ Groundcover

Attracts: _____

Resists: _____

Special Features: _____

Location Placed: _____

Date Planted: _____

Date Germinated: _____

Light Requirements:

☐ Shade ☐ Partial Sun ☐ Sun

Hardiness Zone: _____

Soil Requirements: _____ Watering Requirements: _____

Season of Bloom: _____ Spacing: _____

Plant Width: _____ Plant Height: _____ Root Depth: _____

Care Notes (Pruning/Pest/Weed Control/Propagation/Fertilizer):

_____
_____
_____

Notes: _____
_____
_____
_____
_____

PLANT LOGBOOK

Plant Name (Common): _____

Genus Name: _____

☐ Bulb ☐ Herb ☐ Vegetable ☐ Shrub ☐ Tree ☐ Flower ☐ Indoor

☐ Rhizome ☐ Seedling ☐ Perennial ☐ Annual ☐ Biennial ☐ Outdoor

☐ Tuber ☐ Bare Root ☐ Vine ☐ Ornamental ☐ Fruit ☐ Groundcover

Attracts: _____

Resists: _____

Special Features: _____

Location Placed: _____

Date Planted: _____

Date Germinated: _____

Light Requirements:

☐ Shade ☐ Partial Sun ☐ Sun

Hardiness Zone: _____

Soil Requirements: _____ Watering Requirements: _____

Season of Bloom: _____ Spacing: _____

Plant Width: _____ Plant Height: _____ Root Depth: _____

Care Notes (Pruning/Pest/Weed Control/Propagation/Fertilizer):

_____
_____
_____

Notes: _____
_____
_____
_____
_____

PLANT LOGBOOK

Plant Name (Common): _____

Genus Name: _____

☐ Bulb ☐ Herb ☐ Vegetable ☐ Shrub ☐ Tree ☐ Flower ☐ Indoor

☐ Rhizome ☐ Seedling ☐ Perennial ☐ Annual ☐ Biennial ☐ Outdoor

☐ Tuber ☐ Bare Root ☐ Vine ☐ Ornamental ☐ Fruit ☐ Groundcover

Attracts: _____

Resists: _____

Special Features: _____

Location Placed: _____

Date Planted: _____

Date Germinated: _____

Light Requirements:

☐ Shade ☐ Partial Sun ☐ Sun

Hardiness Zone: _____

Soil Requirements: _____ Watering Requirements: _____

Season of Bloom: _____ Spacing: _____

Plant Width: _____ Plant Height: _____ Root Depth: _____

Care Notes (Pruning/Pest/Weed Control/Propagation/Fertilizer):

_____
_____
_____

Notes: _____
_____
_____
_____
_____

PLANT LOGBOOK

Plant Name (Common): _____

Genus Name: _____

☐ Bulb ☐ Herb ☐ Vegetable ☐ Shrub ☐ Tree ☐ Flower ☐ Indoor

☐ Rhizome ☐ Seedling ☐ Perennial ☐ Annual ☐ Biennial ☐ Outdoor

☐ Tuber ☐ Bare Root ☐ Vine ☐ Ornamental ☐ Fruit ☐ Groundcover

Attracts: _____

Resists: _____

Special Features: _____

Location Placed: _____

Date Planted: _____

Date Germinated: _____

Light Requirements:

☐ Shade ☐ Partial Sun ☐ Sun

Hardiness Zone: _____

Soil Requirements: _____ Watering Requirements: _____

Season of Bloom: _____ Spacing: _____

Plant Width: _____ Plant Height: _____ Root Depth: _____

Care Notes (Pruning/Pest/Weed Control/Propagation/Fertilizer):

_____
_____
_____
_____

Notes: _____
_____
_____
_____
_____

PLANT LOGBOOK

Plant Name (Common): _____

Genus Name: _____

☐ Bulb ☐ Herb ☐ Vegetable ☐ Shrub ☐ Tree ☐ Flower ☐ Indoor

☐ Rhizome ☐ Seedling ☐ Perennial ☐ Annual ☐ Biennial ☐ Outdoor

☐ Tuber ☐ Bare Root ☐ Vine ☐ Ornamental ☐ Fruit ☐ Groundcover

Attracts: _____

Resists: _____

Special Features: _____

Location Placed: _____

Date Planted: _____

Date Germinated: _____

Light Requirements:

☐ Shade ☐ Partial Sun ☐ Sun

Hardiness Zone: _____

Soil Requirements: _____ Watering Requirements: _____

Season of Bloom: _____ Spacing: _____

Plant Width: _____ Plant Height: _____ Root Depth: _____

Care Notes (Pruning/Pest/Weed Control/Propagation/Fertilizer):

_____
_____
_____

Notes: _____
_____
_____
_____
_____

PLANT LOGBOOK

Plant Name (Common): _____

Genus Name: _____

☐ Bulb ☐ Herb ☐ Vegetable ☐ Shrub ☐ Tree ☐ Flower ☐ Indoor

☐ Rhizome ☐ Seedling ☐ Perennial ☐ Annual ☐ Biennial ☐ Outdoor

☐ Tuber ☐ Bare Root ☐ Vine ☐ Ornamental ☐ Fruit ☐ Groundcover

Attracts: _____

Resists: _____

Special Features: _____

Location Placed: _____

Date Planted: _____

Date Germinated: _____

Light Requirements:

☐ Shade ☐ Partial Sun ☐ Sun

Hardiness Zone: _____

Soil Requirements: _____ Watering Requirements: _____

Season of Bloom: _____ Spacing: _____

Plant Width: _____ Plant Height: _____ Root Depth: _____

Care Notes (Pruning/Pest/Weed Control/Propagation/Fertilizer):

_____

_____

_____

Notes: _____

_____

_____

_____

_____

PLANT LOGBOOK

Plant Name (Common): _____

Genus Name: _____

☐ Bulb ☐ Herb ☐ Vegetable ☐ Shrub ☐ Tree ☐ Flower ☐ Indoor

☐ Rhizome ☐ Seedling ☐ Perennial ☐ Annual ☐ Biennial ☐ Outdoor

☐ Tuber ☐ Bare Root ☐ Vine ☐ Ornamental ☐ Fruit ☐ Groundcover

Attracts: _____

Resists: _____

Special Features: _____

Location Placed: _____

Date Planted: _____

Date Germinated: _____

Light Requirements:

☐ Shade ☐ Partial Sun ☐ Sun

Hardiness Zone: _____

Soil Requirements: _____ Watering Requirements: _____

Season of Bloom: _____ Spacing: _____

Plant Width: _____ Plant Height: _____ Root Depth: _____

Care Notes (Pruning/Pest/Weed Control/Propagation/Fertilizer):

_____

_____

_____

Notes: _____

_____

_____

_____

_____

PLANT LOGBOOK

Plant Name (Common): _____

Genus Name: _____

☐ Bulb ☐ Herb ☐ Vegetable ☐ Shrub ☐ Tree ☐ Flower ☐ Indoor

☐ Rhizome ☐ Seedling ☐ Perennial ☐ Annual ☐ Biennial ☐ Outdoor

☐ Tuber ☐ Bare Root ☐ Vine ☐ Ornamental ☐ Fruit ☐ Groundcover

Attracts: _____

Resists: _____

Special Features: _____

Location Placed: _____

Date Planted: _____

Date Germinated: _____

Light Requirements:

☐ Shade ☐ Partial Sun ☐ Sun

Hardiness Zone: _____

Soil Requirements: _____ Watering Requirements: _____

Season of Bloom: _____ Spacing: _____

Plant Width: _____ Plant Height: _____ Root Depth: _____

Care Notes (Pruning/Pest/Weed Control/Propagation/Fertilizer):

_____

_____

_____

Notes: _____

_____

_____

_____

_____

PLANT LOGBOOK

Plant Name (Common): _____

Genus Name: _____

☐ Bulb ☐ Herb ☐ Vegetable ☐ Shrub ☐ Tree ☐ Flower ☐ Indoor

☐ Rhizome ☐ Seedling ☐ Perennial ☐ Annual ☐ Biennial ☐ Outdoor

☐ Tuber ☐ Bare Root ☐ Vine ☐ Ornamental ☐ Fruit ☐ Groundcover

Attracts: _____

Resists: _____

Special Features: _____

Location Placed: _____

Date Planted: _____

Date Germinated: _____

Light Requirements:

☐ Shade ☐ Partial Sun ☐ Sun

Hardiness Zone: _____

Soil Requirements: _____ Watering Requirements: _____

Season of Bloom: _____ Spacing: _____

Plant Width: _____ Plant Height: _____ Root Depth: _____

Care Notes (Pruning/Pest/Weed Control/Propagation/Fertilizer):

_____
_____
_____

Notes: _____
_____
_____
_____
_____

PLANT LOGBOOK

Plant Name (Common): _____

Genus Name: _____

☐ Bulb ☐ Herb ☐ Vegetable ☐ Shrub ☐ Tree ☐ Flower ☐ Indoor

☐ Rhizome ☐ Seedling ☐ Perennial ☐ Annual ☐ Biennial ☐ Outdoor

☐ Tuber ☐ Bare Root ☐ Vine ☐ Ornamental ☐ Fruit ☐ Groundcover

Attracts: _____

Resists: _____

Special Features: _____

Location Placed: _____

Date Planted: _____

Date Germinated: _____

Light Requirements:

☐ Shade ☐ Partial Sun ☐ Sun

Hardiness Zone: _____

Soil Requirements: _____ Watering Requirements: _____

Season of Bloom: _____ Spacing: _____

Plant Width: _____ Plant Height: _____ Root Depth: _____

Care Notes (Pruning/Pest/Weed Control/Propagation/Fertilizer):

_____
_____
_____

Notes: _____
_____
_____
_____
_____

PLANT LOGBOOK

Plant Name (Common): _____

Genus Name: _____

☐ Bulb ☐ Herb ☐ Vegetable ☐ Shrub ☐ Tree ☐ Flower ☐ Indoor

☐ Rhizome ☐ Seedling ☐ Perennial ☐ Annual ☐ Biennial ☐ Outdoor

☐ Tuber ☐ Bare Root ☐ Vine ☐ Ornamental ☐ Fruit ☐ Groundcover

Attracts: _____

Resists: _____

Special Features: _____

Location Placed: _____

Date Planted: _____

Date Germinated: _____

Light Requirements:

☐ Shade ☐ Partial Sun ☐ Sun

Hardiness Zone: _____

Soil Requirements: _____   Watering Requirements: _____

Season of Bloom: _____   Spacing: _____

Plant Width: _____ Plant Height: _____ Root Depth: _____

Care Notes (Pruning/Pest/Weed Control/Propagation/Fertilizer):
_____
_____
_____

Notes: _____
_____
_____
_____
_____

PLANT LOGBOOK

Plant Name (Common): _____

Genus Name: _____

☐ Bulb ☐ Herb ☐ Vegetable ☐ Shrub ☐ Tree ☐ Flower ☐ Indoor

☐ Rhizome ☐ Seedling ☐ Perennial ☐ Annual ☐ Biennial ☐ Outdoor

☐ Tuber ☐ Bare Root ☐ Vine ☐ Ornamental ☐ Fruit ☐ Groundcover

Attracts: _____

Resists: _____

Special Features: _____

Location Placed: _____

Date Planted: _____

Date Germinated: _____

Light Requirements:

☐ Shade ☐ Partial Sun ☐ Sun

Hardiness Zone: _____

Soil Requirements: _____ Watering Requirements: _____

Season of Bloom: _____ Spacing: _____

Plant Width: _____ Plant Height: _____ Root Depth: _____

Care Notes (Pruning/Pest/Weed Control/Propagation/Fertilizer):

_____
_____
_____
_____

Notes: _____
_____
_____
_____
_____

PLANT LOGBOOK

Plant Name (Common): _____

Genus Name: _____

☐ Bulb ☐ Herb ☐ Vegetable ☐ Shrub ☐ Tree ☐ Flower ☐ Indoor

☐ Rhizome ☐ Seedling ☐ Perennial ☐ Annual ☐ Biennial ☐ Outdoor

☐ Tuber ☐ Bare Root ☐ Vine ☐ Ornamental ☐ Fruit ☐ Groundcover

Attracts: _____

Resists: _____

Special Features: _____

Location Placed: _____

Date Planted: _____

Date Germinated: _____

Light Requirements:

☐ Shade ☐ Partial Sun ☐ Sun

Hardiness Zone: _____

Soil Requirements: _____ Watering Requirements: _____

Season of Bloom: _____ Spacing: _____

Plant Width: _____ Plant Height: _____ Root Depth: _____

Care Notes (Pruning/Pest/Weed Control/Propagation/Fertilizer):

_____
_____
_____

Notes: _____
_____
_____
_____
_____

PLANT LOGBOOK

Plant Name (Common): _____

Genus Name: _____

☐ Bulb ☐ Herb ☐ Vegetable ☐ Shrub ☐ Tree ☐ Flower ☐ Indoor

☐ Rhizome ☐ Seedling ☐ Perennial ☐ Annual ☐ Biennial ☐ Outdoor

☐ Tuber ☐ Bare Root ☐ Vine ☐ Ornamental ☐ Fruit ☐ Groundcover

Attracts: _____

Resists: _____

Special Features: _____

Location Placed: _____

Date Planted: _____

Date Germinated: _____

Light Requirements:

☐ Shade ☐ Partial Sun ☐ Sun

Hardiness Zone: _____

Soil Requirements: _____ Watering Requirements: _____

Season of Bloom: _____ Spacing: _____

Plant Width: _____ Plant Height: _____ Root Depth: _____

Care Notes (Pruning/Pest/Weed Control/Propagation/Fertilizer):

_____
_____
_____

Notes: _____
_____
_____
_____
_____

PLANT LOGBOOK

Plant Name (Common): _____

Genus Name: _____

☐ Bulb ☐ Herb ☐ Vegetable ☐ Shrub ☐ Tree ☐ Flower ☐ Indoor

☐ Rhizome ☐ Seedling ☐ Perennial ☐ Annual ☐ Biennial ☐ Outdoor

☐ Tuber ☐ Bare Root ☐ Vine ☐ Ornamental ☐ Fruit ☐ Groundcover

Attracts: _____

Resists: _____

Special Features: _____

Location Placed: _____

Date Planted: _____

Date Germinated: _____

Light Requirements:

☐ Shade ☐ Partial Sun ☐ Sun

Hardiness Zone: _____

Soil Requirements: _____ Watering Requirements: _____

Season of Bloom: _____ Spacing: _____

Plant Width: _____ Plant Height: _____ Root Depth: _____

Care Notes (Pruning/Pest/Weed Control/Propagation/Fertilizer):

_____
_____
_____

Notes: _____
_____
_____
_____
_____

PLANT LOGBOOK

Plant Name (Common): _____

Genus Name: _____

☐ Bulb ☐ Herb ☐ Vegetable ☐ Shrub ☐ Tree ☐ Flower ☐ Indoor

☐ Rhizome ☐ Seedling ☐ Perennial ☐ Annual ☐ Biennial ☐ Outdoor

☐ Tuber ☐ Bare Root ☐ Vine ☐ Ornamental ☐ Fruit ☐ Groundcover

Attracts: _____

Resists: _____

Special Features: _____

Location Placed: _____

Date Planted: _____

Date Germinated: _____

Light Requirements:

☐ Shade ☐ Partial Sun ☐ Sun

Hardiness Zone: _____

Soil Requirements: _____ Watering Requirements: _____

Season of Bloom: _____ Spacing: _____

Plant Width: _____ Plant Height: _____ Root Depth: _____

Care Notes (Pruning/Pest/Weed Control/Propagation/Fertilizer):

_____
_____
_____

Notes: _____
_____
_____
_____
_____

PLANT LOGBOOK

Plant Name (Common): _____

Genus Name: _____

☐ Bulb ☐ Herb ☐ Vegetable ☐ Shrub ☐ Tree ☐ Flower ☐ Indoor

☐ Rhizome ☐ Seedling ☐ Perennial ☐ Annual ☐ Biennial ☐ Outdoor

☐ Tuber ☐ Bare Root ☐ Vine ☐ Ornamental ☐ Fruit ☐ Groundcover

Attracts: _____

Resists: _____

Special Features: _____

Location Placed: _____

Date Planted: _____

Date Germinated: _____

Light Requirements:

☐ Shade ☐ Partial Sun ☐ Sun

Hardiness Zone: _____

Soil Requirements: _____ Watering Requirements: _____

Season of Bloom: _____ Spacing: _____

Plant Width: _____ Plant Height: _____ Root Depth: _____

Care Notes (Pruning/Pest/Weed Control/Propagation/Fertilizer):

_____
_____
_____

Notes: _____
_____
_____
_____
_____

PLANT LOGBOOK

Plant Name (Common): _____

Genus Name: _____

☐ Bulb ☐ Herb ☐ Vegetable ☐ Shrub ☐ Tree ☐ Flower ☐ Indoor

☐ Rhizome ☐ Seedling ☐ Perennial ☐ Annual ☐ Biennial ☐ Outdoor

☐ Tuber ☐ Bare Root ☐ Vine ☐ Ornamental ☐ Fruit ☐ Groundcover

Attracts: _____

Resists: _____

Special Features: _____

Location Placed: _____

Date Planted: _____

Date Germinated: _____

Light Requirements:

☐ Shade ☐ Partial Sun ☐ Sun

Hardiness Zone: _____

Soil Requirements: _____ Watering Requirements: _____

Season of Bloom: _____ Spacing: _____

Plant Width: _____ Plant Height: _____ Root Depth: _____

Care Notes (Pruning/Pest/Weed Control/Propagation/Fertilizer):

_____
_____
_____
_____

Notes: _____
_____
_____
_____
_____

PLANT LOGBOOK

Plant Name (Common): _____

Genus Name: _____

☐ Bulb ☐ Herb ☐ Vegetable ☐ Shrub ☐ Tree ☐ Flower ☐ Indoor

☐ Rhizome ☐ Seedling ☐ Perennial ☐ Annual ☐ Biennial ☐ Outdoor

☐ Tuber ☐ Bare Root ☐ Vine ☐ Ornamental ☐ Fruit ☐ Groundcover

Attracts: _____

Resists: _____

Special Features: _____

Location Placed: _____

Date Planted: _____

Date Germinated: _____

Light Requirements:

☐ Shade ☐ Partial Sun ☐ Sun

Hardiness Zone: _____

Soil Requirements: _____ Watering Requirements: _____

Season of Bloom: _____ Spacing: _____

Plant Width: _____ Plant Height: _____ Root Depth: _____

Care Notes (Pruning/Pest/Weed Control/Propagation/Fertilizer):

_____
_____
_____

Notes: _____
_____
_____
_____
_____

PLANT LOGBOOK

Plant Name (Common): _____

Genus Name: _____

☐ Bulb ☐ Herb ☐ Vegetable ☐ Shrub ☐ Tree ☐ Flower ☐ Indoor

☐ Rhizome ☐ Seedling ☐ Perennial ☐ Annual ☐ Biennial ☐ Outdoor

☐ Tuber ☐ Bare Root ☐ Vine ☐ Ornamental ☐ Fruit ☐ Groundcover

Attracts: _____

Resists: _____

Special Features: _____

Location Placed: _____

Date Planted: _____

Date Germinated: _____

Light Requirements:

☐ Shade ☐ Partial Sun ☐ Sun

Hardiness Zone: _____

Soil Requirements: _____ Watering Requirements: _____

Season of Bloom: _____ Spacing: _____

Plant Width: _____ Plant Height: _____ Root Depth: _____

Care Notes (Pruning/Pest/Weed Control/Propagation/Fertilizer):

_____
_____
_____
_____

Notes: _____
_____
_____
_____
_____

PLANT LOGBOOK

Plant Name (Common): _____

Genus Name: _____

☐ Bulb ☐ Herb ☐ Vegetable ☐ Shrub ☐ Tree ☐ Flower ☐ Indoor

☐ Rhizome ☐ Seedling ☐ Perennial ☐ Annual ☐ Biennial ☐ Outdoor

☐ Tuber ☐ Bare Root ☐ Vine ☐ Ornamental ☐ Fruit ☐ Groundcover

Attracts: _____

Resists: _____

Special Features: _____

Location Placed: _____

Date Planted: _____

Date Germinated: _____

Light Requirements:

☐ Shade ☐ Partial Sun ☐ Sun

Hardiness Zone: _____

Soil Requirements: _____ Watering Requirements: _____

Season of Bloom: _____ Spacing: _____

Plant Width: _____ Plant Height: _____ Root Depth: _____

Care Notes (Pruning/Pest/Weed Control/Propagation/Fertilizer):

_____
_____
_____

Notes: _____
_____
_____
_____
_____

PLANT LOGBOOK

Plant Name (Common): _____

Genus Name: _____

☐ Bulb ☐ Herb ☐ Vegetable ☐ Shrub ☐ Tree ☐ Flower ☐ Indoor

☐ Rhizome ☐ Seedling ☐ Perennial ☐ Annual ☐ Biennial ☐ Outdoor

☐ Tuber ☐ Bare Root ☐ Vine ☐ Ornamental ☐ Fruit ☐ Groundcover

Attracts: _____

Resists: _____

Special Features: _____

Location Placed: _____

Date Planted: _____

Date Germinated: _____

Light Requirements:

☐ Shade ☐ Partial Sun ☐ Sun

Hardiness Zone: _____

Soil Requirements: _____ Watering Requirements: _____

Season of Bloom: _____ Spacing: _____

Plant Width: _____ Plant Height: _____ Root Depth: _____

Care Notes (Pruning/Pest/Weed Control/Propagation/Fertilizer):

_____
_____
_____

Notes: _____
_____
_____
_____
_____

PLANT LOGBOOK

Plant Name (Common): _____

Genus Name: _____

☐ Bulb ☐ Herb ☐ Vegetable ☐ Shrub ☐ Tree ☐ Flower ☐ Indoor

☐ Rhizome ☐ Seedling ☐ Perennial ☐ Annual ☐ Biennial ☐ Outdoor

☐ Tuber ☐ Bare Root ☐ Vine ☐ Ornamental ☐ Fruit ☐ Groundcover

Attracts: _____

Resists: _____

Special Features: _____

Location Placed: _____

Date Planted: _____

Date Germinated: _____

Light Requirements:

☐ Shade ☐ Partial Sun ☐ Sun

Hardiness Zone: _____

Soil Requirements: _____ Watering Requirements: _____

Season of Bloom: _____ Spacing: _____

Plant Width: _____ Plant Height: _____ Root Depth: _____

Care Notes (Pruning/Pest/Weed Control/Propagation/Fertilizer):

_____
_____
_____

Notes: _____
_____
_____
_____
_____

PLANT LOGBOOK

Plant Name (Common): _____

Genus Name: _____

☐ Bulb ☐ Herb ☐ Vegetable ☐ Shrub ☐ Tree ☐ Flower ☐ Indoor

☐ Rhizome ☐ Seedling ☐ Perennial ☐ Annual ☐ Biennial ☐ Outdoor

☐ Tuber ☐ Bare Root ☐ Vine ☐ Ornamental ☐ Fruit ☐ Groundcover

Attracts: _____

Resists: _____

Special Features: _____

Location Placed: _____

Date Planted: _____

Date Germinated: _____

Light Requirements:

☐ Shade ☐ Partial Sun ☐ Sun

Hardiness Zone: _____

Soil Requirements: _____ Watering Requirements: _____

Season of Bloom: _____ Spacing: _____

Plant Width: _____ Plant Height: _____ Root Depth: _____

Care Notes (Pruning/Pest/Weed Control/Propagation/Fertilizer):

_____
_____
_____

Notes: _____
_____
_____
_____
_____

PLANT LOGBOOK

Plant Name (Common): _____

Genus Name: _____

☐ Bulb ☐ Herb ☐ Vegetable ☐ Shrub ☐ Tree ☐ Flower ☐ Indoor

☐ Rhizome ☐ Seedling ☐ Perennial ☐ Annual ☐ Biennial ☐ Outdoor

☐ Tuber ☐ Bare Root ☐ Vine ☐ Ornamental ☐ Fruit ☐ Groundcover

Attracts: _____

Resists: _____

Special Features: _____

Location Placed: _____

Date Planted: _____

Date Germinated: _____

Light Requirements:

☐ Shade ☐ Partial Sun ☐ Sun

Hardiness Zone: _____

Soil Requirements: _____ Watering Requirements: _____

Season of Bloom: _____ Spacing: _____

Plant Width: _____ Plant Height: _____ Root Depth: _____

Care Notes (Pruning/Pest/Weed Control/Propagation/Fertilizer):

_____

_____

_____

Notes: _____

_____

_____

_____

_____

PLANT LOGBOOK

Plant Name (Common): _____

Genus Name: _____

☐ Bulb ☐ Herb ☐ Vegetable ☐ Shrub ☐ Tree ☐ Flower ☐ Indoor

☐ Rhizome ☐ Seedling ☐ Perennial ☐ Annual ☐ Biennial ☐ Outdoor

☐ Tuber ☐ Bare Root ☐ Vine ☐ Ornamental ☐ Fruit ☐ Groundcover

Attracts: _____

Resists: _____

Special Features: _____

Location Placed: _____

Date Planted: _____

Date Germinated: _____

Light Requirements:

☐ Shade ☐ Partial Sun ☐ Sun

Hardiness Zone: _____

Soil Requirements: _____ Watering Requirements: _____

Season of Bloom: _____ Spacing: _____

Plant Width: _____ Plant Height: _____ Root Depth: _____

Care Notes (Pruning/Pest/Weed Control/Propagation/Fertilizer):

_____

_____

_____

Notes: _____

_____

_____

_____

_____

PLANT LOGBOOK

Plant Name (Common): _____

Genus Name: _____

☐ Bulb ☐ Herb ☐ Vegetable ☐ Shrub ☐ Tree ☐ Flower ☐ Indoor

☐ Rhizome ☐ Seedling ☐ Perennial ☐ Annual ☐ Biennial ☐ Outdoor

☐ Tuber ☐ Bare Root ☐ Vine ☐ Ornamental ☐ Fruit ☐ Groundcover

Attracts: _____

Resists: _____

Special Features: _____

Location Placed: _____

Date Planted: _____

Date Germinated: _____

Light Requirements:

☐ Shade ☐ Partial Sun ☐ Sun

Hardiness Zone: _____

Soil Requirements: _____ Watering Requirements: _____

Season of Bloom: _____ Spacing: _____

Plant Width: _____ Plant Height: _____ Root Depth: _____

Care Notes (Pruning/Pest/Weed Control/Propagation/Fertilizer):

_____
_____
_____

Notes: _____
_____
_____
_____

PLANT LOGBOOK

Plant Name (Common): _____

Genus Name: _____

☐ Bulb ☐ Herb ☐ Vegetable ☐ Shrub ☐ Tree ☐ Flower ☐ Indoor

☐ Rhizome ☐ Seedling ☐ Perennial ☐ Annual ☐ Biennial ☐ Outdoor

☐ Tuber ☐ Bare Root ☐ Vine ☐ Ornamental ☐ Fruit ☐ Groundcover

Attracts: _____

Resists: _____

Special Features: _____

Location Placed: _____

Date Planted: _____

Date Germinated: _____

Light Requirements:

☐ Shade ☐ Partial Sun ☐ Sun

Hardiness Zone: _____

Soil Requirements: _____ Watering Requirements: _____

Season of Bloom: _____ Spacing: _____

Plant Width: _____ Plant Height: _____ Root Depth: _____

Care Notes (Pruning/Pest/Weed Control/Propagation/Fertilizer):

_____
_____
_____
_____

Notes: _____
_____
_____
_____
_____

PLANT LOGBOOK

Plant Name (Common): _____

Genus Name: _____

☐ Bulb ☐ Herb ☐ Vegetable ☐ Shrub ☐ Tree ☐ Flower ☐ Indoor

☐ Rhizome ☐ Seedling ☐ Perennial ☐ Annual ☐ Biennial ☐ Outdoor

☐ Tuber ☐ Bare Root ☐ Vine ☐ Ornamental ☐ Fruit ☐ Groundcover

Attracts: _____

Resists: _____

Special Features: _____

Location Placed: _____

Date Planted: _____

Date Germinated: _____

Light Requirements:

☐ Shade ☐ Partial Sun ☐ Sun

Hardiness Zone: _____

Soil Requirements: _____ Watering Requirements: _____

Season of Bloom: _____ Spacing: _____

Plant Width: _____ Plant Height: _____ Root Depth: _____

Care Notes (Pruning/Pest/Weed Control/Propagation/Fertilizer):

_____
_____
_____

Notes: _____
_____
_____
_____
_____

PLANT LOGBOOK

Plant Name (Common): _____

Genus Name: _____

☐ Bulb ☐ Herb ☐ Vegetable ☐ Shrub ☐ Tree ☐ Flower ☐ Indoor

☐ Rhizome ☐ Seedling ☐ Perennial ☐ Annual ☐ Biennial ☐ Outdoor

☐ Tuber ☐ Bare Root ☐ Vine ☐ Ornamental ☐ Fruit ☐ Groundcover

Attracts: _____

Resists: _____

Special Features: _____

Location Placed: _____

Date Planted: _____

Date Germinated: _____

Light Requirements:

☐ Shade ☐ Partial Sun ☐ Sun

Hardiness Zone: _____

Soil Requirements: _____ Watering Requirements: _____

Season of Bloom: _____ Spacing: _____

Plant Width: _____ Plant Height: _____ Root Depth: _____

Care Notes (Pruning/Pest/Weed Control/Propagation/Fertilizer):

_____
_____
_____

Notes: _____
_____
_____
_____
_____

CONTAINER DESIGNER

HOW TO USE

Container Designer Sheets

Use this section of the book to plan and design containers on the inside and outside of your home:

◇ Keep track of all the different plant combinations that work well in each container or hanging basket, so what works well can be repeated from season to season

◇ Plan the color scheme so that it can showcase and complement the color of the container for maximum impact

◇ Sketch or insert a photo of the container with some of the plants to provide a reminder for years to come

CONTAINER DESIGNER

Container: _____

☐ Indoor   ☐ Outdoor

Container Details

Shape: _____

Material: _____

Color: _____

Size/Type: ☐ Tall ☐ Med. ☐ Short

☐ Hanging Basket

Drainage Hole: ☐ Yes ☐ No

Location: _____

Height: _____

Best plants to compliment container: _____
_____
_____

Plants	Season	Comments:

Notes: _____
_____
_____

CONTAINER DESIGNER

Container: _____

☐ Indoor   ☐ Outdoor

Container Details

Shape: _____

Material: _____

Color: _____

Size/Type: ☐Tall ☐Med. ☐Short

☐Hanging Basket

Drainage Hole: ☐ Yes   ☐ No

Location: _____

Height: _____

Best plants to compliment container: _____
_____
_____

Plants	Season	Comments:
_____	_____	_____
_____	_____	_____
_____	_____	_____
_____	_____	_____
_____	_____	_____
_____	_____	_____
_____	_____	_____
_____	_____	_____
_____	_____	_____

Notes: _____
_____
_____

CONTAINER DESIGNER

Container: _____

☐ Indoor   ☐ Outdoor

Container Details

Shape: _____

Material: _____

Color: _____

Size/Type: ☐ Tall ☐ Med. ☐ Short

☐ Hanging Basket

Drainage Hole: ☐ Yes   ☐ No

Location: _____

Height: _____

Best plants to compliment container: _____
_____
_____

Plants	Season	Comments:
_____	_____	_____
_____	_____	_____
_____	_____	_____
_____	_____	_____
_____	_____	_____
_____	_____	_____
_____	_____	_____
_____	_____	_____
_____	_____	_____

Notes: _____
_____
_____

CONTAINER DESIGNER

Container: _____

☐ Indoor   ☐ Outdoor

Container Details

Shape: _____

Material: _____

Color: _____

Size/Type: ☐ Tall ☐ Med. ☐ Short

                   ☐ Hanging Basket

Drainage Hole: ☐ Yes   ☐ No

Location: _____

Height: _____

Best plants to compliment container: _____
_____
_____

Plants	Season	Comments:

Notes: _____
_____
_____

CONTAINER DESIGNER

Container: _____

☐ Indoor ☐ Outdoor

Container Details

Shape: _____

Material: _____

Color: _____

Size/Type: ☐ Tall ☐ Med. ☐ Short

☐ Hanging Basket

Drainage Hole: ☐ Yes ☐ No

Location: _____

Height: _____

Best plants to compliment container: _____
_____
_____

Plants	Season	Comments:

Notes: _____
_____
_____

CONTAINER DESIGNER

Container: _____

☐ Indoor   ☐ Outdoor

Container Details

Shape: _____

Material: _____

Color: _____

Size/Type: ☐ Tall ☐ Med. ☐ Short

           ☐ Hanging Basket

Drainage Hole: ☐ Yes ☐ No

Location: _____

Height: _____

Best plants to compliment container: _____
_____
_____

Plants	Season	Comments:

Notes: _____
_____
_____

CONTAINER DESIGNER

Container: _____

☐ Indoor ☐ Outdoor

Container Details

Shape: _____

Material: _____

Color: _____

Size/Type: ☐ Tall ☐ Med. ☐ Short

☐ Hanging Basket

Drainage Hole: ☐ Yes ☐ No

Location: _____

Height: _____

Best plants to compliment container: _____
_____
_____

Plants	Season	Comments:

Notes: _____
_____

CONTAINER DESIGNER

Container: _____

☐ Indoor ☐ Outdoor

Container Details

Shape: _____

Material: _____

Color: _____

Size/Type: ☐ Tall ☐ Med. ☐ Short

☐ Hanging Basket

Drainage Hole: ☐ Yes ☐ No

Location: _____

Height: _____

Best plants to compliment container: _____
_____
_____

Plants	Season	Comments:

Notes: _____
_____
_____

CONTAINER DESIGNER

Container: _____

☐ Indoor   ☐ Outdoor

Container Details

Shape: _____

Material: _____

Color: _____

Size/Type: ☐ Tall ☐ Med. ☐ Short

☐ Hanging Basket

Drainage Hole: ☐ Yes   ☐ No

Location: _____

Height: _____

Best plants to compliment container: _____
_____
_____

Plants	Season	Comments:

Notes: _____
_____
_____

CONTAINER DESIGNER

Container: _____

☐ Indoor   ☐ Outdoor

Container Details

Shape: _____

Material: _____

Color: _____

Size/Type: ☐ Tall ☐ Med. ☐ Short

☐ Hanging Basket

Drainage Hole: ☐ Yes   ☐ No

Location: _____

Height: _____

Best plants to compliment container: _____
_____
_____

Plants	Season	Comments:

Notes: _____
_____
_____

CONTAINER DESIGNER

Container: _____

☐ Indoor   ☐ Outdoor

Container Details

Shape: _____

Material: _____

Color: _____

Size/Type: ☐ Tall ☐ Med. ☐ Short

☐ Hanging Basket

Drainage Hole: ☐ Yes   ☐ No

Location: _____

Height: _____

Best plants to compliment container: _____
_____
_____

Plants	Season	Comments:

Notes: _____
_____
_____

CONTAINER DESIGNER

Container: _____

☐ Indoor   ☐ Outdoor

Container Details

Shape: _____

Material: _____

Color: _____

Size/Type: ☐ Tall ☐ Med. ☐ Short

☐ Hanging Basket

Drainage Hole: ☐ Yes   ☐ No

Location: _____

Height: _____

Best plants to compliment container: _____

_____

_____

Plants	Season	Comments:

Notes: _____

_____

_____

CONTAINER DESIGNER

Container: _____

☐ Indoor   ☐ Outdoor

Container Details

Shape: _____

Material: _____

Color: _____

Size/Type: ☐ Tall ☐ Med. ☐ Short

☐ Hanging Basket

Drainage Hole: ☐ Yes   ☐ No

Location: _____

Height: _____

Best plants to compliment container: _____
_____
_____

Plants	Season	Comments:

Notes: _____
_____

CONTAINER DESIGNER

Container: _____

☐ Indoor ☐ Outdoor

Container Details

Shape: _____

Material: _____

Color: _____

Size/Type: ☐ Tall ☐ Med. ☐ Short

☐ Hanging Basket

Drainage Hole: ☐ Yes ☐ No

Location: _____

Height: _____

Best plants to compliment container: _____
_____
_____

Plants	Season	Comments:
_____	_____	_____
_____	_____	_____
_____	_____	_____
_____	_____	_____
_____	_____	_____
_____	_____	_____
_____	_____	_____
_____	_____	_____
_____	_____	_____

Notes: _____
_____
_____

CONTAINER DESIGNER

Container: _____

☐ Indoor   ☐ Outdoor

Container Details

Shape: _____

Material: _____

Color: _____

Size/Type: ☐ Tall ☐ Med. ☐ Short

☐ Hanging Basket

Drainage Hole: ☐ Yes   ☐ No

Location: _____

Height: _____

Best plants to compliment container: _____
_____
_____

Plants	Season	Comments:

Notes: _____
_____
_____

CONTAINER DESIGNER

Container: _____

☐ Indoor   ☐ Outdoor

Container Details

Shape: _____

Material: _____

Color: _____

Size/Type: ☐ Tall ☐ Med. ☐ Short

☐ Hanging Basket

Drainage Hole: ☐ Yes   ☐ No

Location: _____

Height: _____

Best plants to compliment container: _____
_____
_____

Plants	Season	Comments:

Notes: _____
_____
_____

CONTAINER DESIGNER

Container: _____

☐ Indoor   ☐ Outdoor

Container Details

Shape: _____

Material: _____

Color: _____

Size/Type: ☐ Tall ☐ Med. ☐ Short

☐ Hanging Basket

Drainage Hole: ☐ Yes   ☐ No

Location: _____

Height: _____

Best plants to compliment container: _____
_____
_____

Plants	Season	Comments:

Notes: _____
_____
_____

CONTAINER DESIGNER

Container: _____

☐ Indoor   ☐ Outdoor

Container Details

Shape: _____

Material: _____

Color: _____

Size/Type: ☐ Tall ☐ Med. ☐ Short

☐ Hanging Basket

Drainage Hole: ☐ Yes   ☐ No

Location: _____

Height: _____

Best plants to compliment container: _____

_____

_____

Plants	Season	Comments:

Notes: _____

_____

CONTAINER DESIGNER

Container: _____

☐ Indoor   ☐ Outdoor

Container Details

Shape: _____

Material: _____

Color: _____

Size/Type: ☐ Tall ☐ Med. ☐ Short

☐ Hanging Basket

Drainage Hole: ☐ Yes ☐ No

Location: _____

Height: _____

Best plants to compliment container: _____
_____
_____

Plants	Season	Comments:
_____	_____	_____
_____	_____	_____
_____	_____	_____
_____	_____	_____
_____	_____	_____
_____	_____	_____
_____	_____	_____
_____	_____	_____
_____	_____	_____

Notes: _____
_____
_____

CONTAINER DESIGNER

Container: _____

☐ Indoor   ☐ Outdoor

Container Details

Shape: _____

Material: _____

Color: _____

Size/Type: ☐ Tall ☐ Med. ☐ Short

☐ Hanging Basket

Drainage Hole: ☐ Yes   ☐ No

Location: _____

Height: _____

Best plants to compliment container: _____
_____
_____

Plants	Season	Comments:
_____	_____	_____
_____	_____	_____
_____	_____	_____
_____	_____	_____
_____	_____	_____
_____	_____	_____
_____	_____	_____
_____	_____	_____

Notes: _____
_____
_____

CONTAINER DESIGNER

Container: _____

☐ Indoor ☐ Outdoor

Container Details

Shape: _____

Material: _____

Color: _____

Size/Type: ☐ Tall ☐ Med. ☐ Short

☐ Hanging Basket

Drainage Hole: ☐ Yes ☐ No

Location: _____

Height: _____

Best plants to compliment container: _____

Plants	Season	Comments:

Notes: _____

CONTAINER DESIGNER

Container: _____

☐ Indoor   ☐ Outdoor

Container Details

Shape: _____

Material: _____

Color: _____

Size/Type: ☐ Tall ☐ Med. ☐ Short

☐ Hanging Basket

Drainage Hole: ☐ Yes   ☐ No

Location: _____

Height: _____

Best plants to compliment container: _____
_____
_____

Plants	Season	Comments:

Notes: _____
_____
_____

CONTAINER DESIGNER

Container: _____

☐ Indoor   ☐ Outdoor

Container Details

Shape: _____

Material: _____

Color: _____

Size/Type: ☐ Tall ☐ Med. ☐ Short

☐ Hanging Basket

Drainage Hole: ☐ Yes   ☐ No

Location: _____

Height: _____

Best plants to compliment container: _____
_____
_____

Plants	Season	Comments:
_____	_____	_____
_____	_____	_____
_____	_____	_____
_____	_____	_____
_____	_____	_____
_____	_____	_____
_____	_____	_____
_____	_____	_____
_____	_____	_____

Notes: _____
_____
_____

CONTAINER DESIGNER

Container: _____

☐ Indoor   ☐ Outdoor

Container Details

Shape: _____

Material: _____

Color: _____

Size/Type: ☐ Tall ☐ Med. ☐ Short

              ☐ Hanging Basket

Drainage Hole: ☐ Yes   ☐ No

Location: _____

Height: _____

Best plants to compliment container: _____
_____
_____

Plants	Season	Comments:

Notes: _____
_____
_____

CONTAINER DESIGNER

Container: _____

☐ Indoor   ☐ Outdoor

Container Details

Shape: _____

Material: _____

Color: _____

Size/Type: ☐ Tall ☐ Med. ☐ Short

☐ Hanging Basket

Drainage Hole: ☐ Yes   ☐ No

Location: _____

Height: _____

Best plants to compliment container: _____
_____
_____

Plants	Season	Comments:

Notes: _____
_____
_____

CONTAINER DESIGNER

Container: _____

☐ Indoor ☐ Outdoor

Container Details

Shape: _____

Material: _____

Color: _____

Size/Type: ☐ Tall ☐ Med. ☐ Short

☐ Hanging Basket

Drainage Hole: ☐ Yes ☐ No

Location: _____

Height: _____

Best plants to compliment container: _____
_____
_____

Plants	Season	Comments:

Notes: _____
_____

CONTAINER DESIGNER

Container: _____

☐ Indoor   ☐ Outdoor

Container Details

Shape: _____

Material: _____

Color: _____

Size/Type: ☐ Tall ☐ Med. ☐ Short

☐ Hanging Basket

Drainage Hole: ☐ Yes   ☐ No

Location: _____

Height: _____

Best plants to compliment container: _____
_____
_____

Plants	Season	Comments:

Notes: _____
_____
_____

CONTAINER DESIGNER

Container: _____

☐ Indoor   ☐ Outdoor

Container Details

Shape: _____

Material: _____

Color: _____

Size/Type: ☐ Tall ☐ Med. ☐ Short

☐ Hanging Basket

Drainage Hole: ☐ Yes   ☐ No

Location: _____

Height: _____

Best plants to compliment container: _____

_____

_____

Plants	Season	Comments:

Notes: _____

_____

_____

CONTAINER DESIGNER

Container: _____

☐ Indoor   ☐ Outdoor

Container Details

Shape: _____

Material: _____

Color: _____

Size/Type: ☐ Tall ☐ Med. ☐ Short

☐ Hanging Basket

Drainage Hole: ☐ Yes ☐ No

Location: _____

Height: _____

Best plants to compliment container: _____
_____
_____

Plants	Season	Comments:

Notes: _____
_____
_____

CONTAINER DESIGNER

Container: _____

☐ Indoor　　　☐ Outdoor

Container Details

Shape: _____

Material: _____

Color: _____

Size/Type: ☐ Tall ☐ Med. ☐ Short

☐ Hanging Basket

Drainage Hole: ☐ Yes ☐ No

Location: _____

Height: _____

Best plants to compliment container: _____
_____

Plants	Season	Comments:

Notes: _____
_____

SCHEDULER

HOW TO USE

Scheduler Sheets

This Scheduler section of the book is flexible and can be used to keep track of many year-round activities:

◇ Garden Maintenance — when to prune, mulch, or fertilize

◇ Blooming — Fruit/Harvest periods

◇ Planting Tasks — when to plant Vegetable Seeds, Bulbs, Tubers

◇ Show Color/Flowering Activity to ensure that there is something interesting happening in the garden all the time

◇ Check the box to indicate how you want to use these Scheduler Sheets

◇ Shade the weeks/months that apply

SCHEDULER

☐ Maintenance
☐ Planting

☐ Blooming, Fruit & Harvest
☐ Garden Activity

Description	Jan.	Feb.	Mar.	Apr.	May	June	July	Aug.	Sep.	Oct.	Nov.	Dec.	Notes

SCHEDULER

☐ Maintenance
☐ Planting
☐ Blooming, Fruit & Harvest
☐ Garden Activity

Description	Jan.	Feb.	Mar.	Apr.	May	June	July	Aug.	Sep.	Oct.	Nov.	Dec.	Notes

SCHEDULER

Description	Jan.	Feb.	Mar.	Apr.	May	June	July	Aug.	Sep.	Oct.	Nov.	Dec.	Notes

☐ Maintenance
☐ Planting

☐ Blooming, Fruit & Harvest
☐ Garden Activity

SCHEDULER

Description	Jan.	Feb.	Mar.	Apr.	May	June	July	Aug.	Sep.	Oct.	Nov.	Dec.	Notes

☐ Maintenance
☐ Planting

☐ Blooming, Fruit & Harvest
☐ Garden Activity

SCHEDULER

☐ Maintenance
☐ Planting

☐ Blooming, Fruit & Harvest
☐ Garden Activity

Description	Jan.	Feb.	Mar.	Apr.	May	June	July	Aug.	Sep.	Oct.	Nov.	Dec.	Notes

SCHEDULER

Checkboxes: ☐ Maintenance ☐ Planting ☐ Blooming, Fruit & Harvest ☐ Garden Activity

Description	Jan.	Feb.	Mar.	Apr.	May	June	July	Aug.	Sep.	Oct.	Nov.	Dec.	Notes

SCHEDULER

☐ Maintenance ☐ Blooming, Fruit & Harvest
☐ Planting   ☐ Garden Activity

Description	Jan.	Feb.	Mar.	Apr.	May	June	July	Aug.	Sep.	Oct.	Nov.	Dec.	Notes

SCHEDULER

☐ Maintenance
☐ Planting

☐ Blooming, Fruit & Harvest
☐ Garden Activity

Description	Jan.	Feb.	Mar.	Apr.	May	June	July	Aug.	Sep.	Oct.	Nov.	Dec.	Notes

SCHEDULER

Maintenance ☐
Planting ☐

Blooming, Fruit & Harvest ☐
Garden Activity ☐

Description	Jan.	Feb.	Mar.	Apr.	May	June	July	Aug.	Sep.	Oct.	Nov.	Dec.	Notes

SCHEDULER

☐ Maintenance
☐ Planting
☐ Blooming, Fruit & Harvest
☐ Garden Activity

Description	Jan.	Feb.	Mar.	Apr.	May	June	July	Aug.	Sep.	Oct.	Nov.	Dec.	Notes

SCHEDULER

☐ Maintenance
☐ Planting
☐ Blooming, Fruit & Harvest
☐ Garden Activity

Description	Jan.	Feb.	Mar.	Apr.	May	June	July	Aug.	Sep.	Oct.	Nov.	Dec.	Notes

SCHEDULER

☐ Maintenance
☐ Planting
☐ Blooming, Fruit & Harvest
☐ Garden Activity

Description	Jan.	Feb.	Mar.	Apr.	May	June	July	Aug.	Sep.	Oct.	Nov.	Dec.	Notes

SCHEDULER

Maintenance ☐
Planting ☐

Blooming, Fruit & Harvest ☐
Garden Activity ☐

Description	Jan.	Feb.	Mar.	Apr.	May	June	July	Aug.	Sep.	Oct.	Nov.	Dec.	Notes

SCHEDULER

☐ Maintenance
☐ Planting

☐ Blooming, Fruit & Harvest
☐ Garden Activity

Description	Jan.	Feb.	Mar.	Apr.	May	June	July	Aug.	Sep.	Oct.	Nov.	Dec.	Notes

SCHEDULER

☐ Maintenance
☐ Planting
☐ Blooming, Fruit & Harvest
☐ Garden Activity

Description	Jan.	Feb.	Mar.	Apr.	May	June	July	Aug.	Sep.	Oct.	Nov.	Dec.	Notes

SCHEDULER

☐ Maintenance   ☐ Blooming, Fruit & Harvest
☐ Planting   ☐ Garden Activity

Description	Jan.	Feb.	Mar.	Apr.	May	June	July	Aug.	Sep.	Oct.	Nov.	Dec.	Notes

SCHEDULER

☐ Maintenance
☐ Planting

☐ Blooming, Fruit & Harvest
☐ Garden Activity

Description	Jan.	Feb.	Mar.	Apr.	May	June	July	Aug.	Sep.	Oct.	Nov.	Dec.	Notes

SCHEDULER

☐ Maintenance
☐ Planting
☐ Blooming, Fruit & Harvest
☐ Garden Activity

Description	Jan.	Feb.	Mar.	Apr.	May	June	July	Aug.	Sep.	Oct.	Nov.	Dec.	Notes

SCHEDULER

Maintenance
Planting

Blooming, Fruit & Harvest
Garden Activity

Description	Jan.	Feb.	Mar.	Apr.	May	June	July	Aug.	Sep.	Oct.	Nov.	Dec.	Notes

SCHEDULER

☐ Maintenance
☐ Planting
☐ Blooming, Fruit & Harvest
☐ Garden Activity

Description	Jan.	Feb.	Mar.	Apr.	May	June	July	Aug.	Sep.	Oct.	Nov.	Dec.	Notes

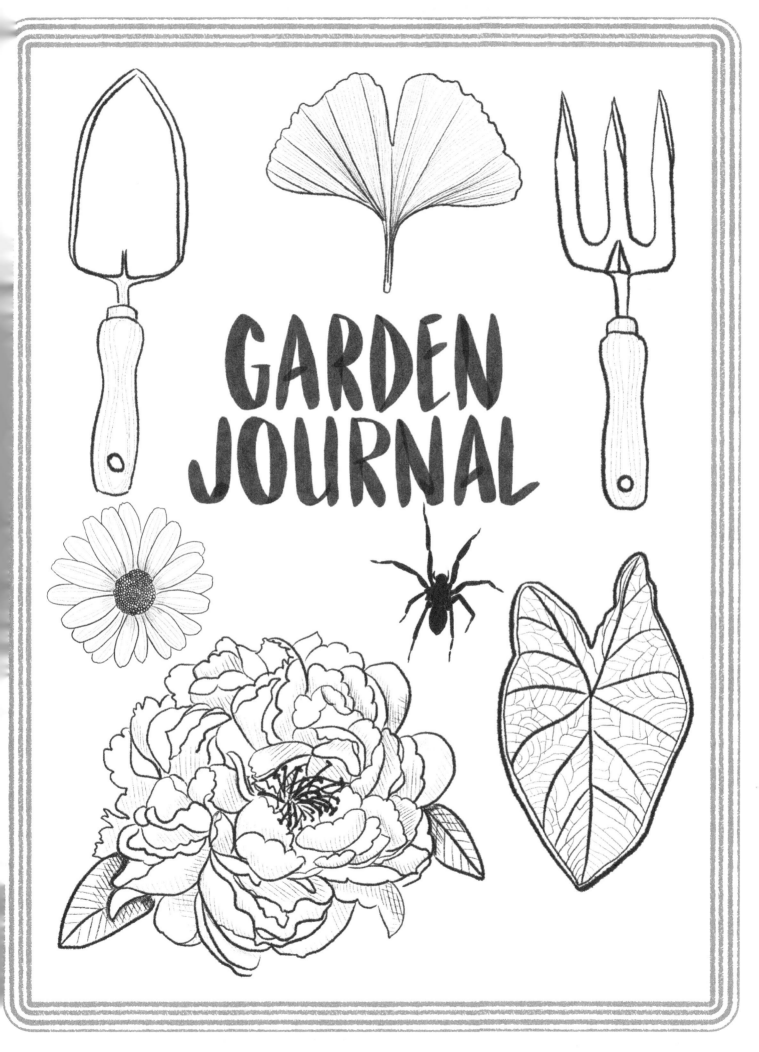

GARDEN JOURNAL

HOW TO USE

Journal Entries

This is a place to journal about all things gardening. Comes with inspirational, garden-specific quotes. You can also use this place in the book to:

◇ Keep track of gardening activities

◇ List things to try or remember ideas for next year

◇ Record what was learned from other gardens or from your local flower and garden show

◇ Journal and self reflect in the surroundings of your own garden

HAPPINESS IS WATCHING YOUR PLANT GROW

TO PLANT A GARDEN IS TO BELIEVE IN TOMORROW
-AUDREY HEPBURN

BLOOM WHERE YOU ARE PLANTED

LIFE BEGINS THE DAY YOU START A GARDEN

A GARDEN IS A FRIEND YOU CAN VISIT ANYTIME

COUNT THE GARDEN BY THE FLOWERS,
NOT BY THE LEAVES THAT FALL

MY GARDEN IS MY MOST
BEAUTIFUL MASTERPIECE

GARDENING ADDS YEARS TO YOUR LIFE
AND LIFE TO YOUR YEARS

MONEY CAN'T BUY HAPPINESS
EXCEPT AT A GARDEN CENTER

THERE IS NO PLACE LIKE MY GARDEN

EVERY FLOWER IS LIKE A SOUL
BLOSSOMING IN NATURE

THE BEST TIME TO GROW A TREE WAS 20 YEARS AGO,
THE SECOND BEST TIME IS NOW

HAPPINESS IS TO HOLD FLOWERS IN BOTH HANDS

MORE GROWS IN THE GARDEN
THAN THE GARDENER SOWS

STOP AND SMELL THE ROSES

Wink Eye Press is based in Vancouver, Canada
and specializes in printed goods. At Wink Eye
Press, we prioritize beauty and function — our
combined technical and artistic backgrounds
create curated goods that are not only useful,
but also appealing. All of our creations are
originally conceptualized, thoughtfully
designed, and illustrated in house.

Every day is an adventure — make life exciting!

wink eye press

Thank you for your purchase

For more books, please visit us at:
www.winkeyepress.com